A COMPACT
GUIDE
TO THE
CHRISTIAN
LIFE

A COMPACT
GUIDE
TO THE
CHRISTIAN
LIFE

KAREN LEE-THORP

NAVPRESS
Discipleship Inside Out®

Discipleship Inside Out®

NavPress is the publishing ministry of The Navigators, an international Christian organization and leader in personal spiritual development. NavPress is committed to helping people grow spiritually and enjoy lives of meaning and hope through personal and group resources that are biblically rooted, culturally relevant, and highly practical.

For a free catalog go to www.NavPress.com
or call 1.800.366.7788 in the United States or 1.800.839.4769 in Canada.

© 1989, 2001, 2013 by The Navigators

ISBN-13: 978-1-61291-413-8

Cover design by Arvid Wallen
Cover images by Shutterstock

Some of the anecdotal illustrations in this book are true to life and are included with the permission of the persons involved. All other illustrations are composites of real situations, and any resemblance to people living or dead is coincidental.

Unless otherwise identified, all Scripture quotations in this publication are taken from the *Holy Bible, New International Version*® (NIV®). Copyright © 1973, 1978, 1984 by Biblica, used by permission of Zondervan. All rights reserved. Other versions used include: the New American Standard Bible® (NASB), Copyright © 1960, 1962, 1963, 1968, 1971, 1972, 1973, 1975, 1977, 1995 by The Lockman Foundation. Used by permission; *The Living Bible* (TLB), copyright © 1971, used by permission of Tyndale House Publishers, Inc., Wheaton, IL 60189, all rights reserved; the *Holy Bible*, New Living Translation (NLT), copyright © 1996, 2004. Used by permission of Tyndale House Publishers, Inc., Wheaton, Illinois 60189. All rights reserved; and the King James Version (KJV).

Lee-Thorp, Karen.
  A compact guide to the Christian life / Karen Lee-Thorp.
    pages cm
  Includes bibliographical references.
  ISBN 978-1-61291-413-8
  1. Christian life. I. Title.
  BV4501.3.L44 2013
  248.4—dc23

                        2012050144

Printed in the United States of America

1 2 3 4 5 6 7 8 / 18 17 16 15 14 13

CONTENTS

THE BODY OF CHRIST

LIFE IN THE WORLD

INTRODUCTION

WHAT IS A DISCIPLE?

The Sovereign LORD has given me an instructed tongue,
>   to know the word that sustains the weary.
He wakens me morning by morning,
>   wakens my ear to listen like one being taught. (Isaiah 50:4)

The word *disciple* means "learner." In Jesus' day, a person who wanted to learn wisdom would follow a teacher around, listen to him teach, and watch him live. The disciple's goal was not just to learn facts from his master but to become like him in every aspect. Thus, a disciple of Jesus is someone who *follows Him in order to become just like Him.* Discipleship is a matter of *being with* and *being like* more than a matter of following rules. But in addition, the disciple is:

- Under Jesus' authority in every area
- Actively seeking to learn His teaching
- Actively seeking to do what He does

Learning and obeying are essential, but they must flow from a growing, intimate relationship with the Master.

In the following pages, you'll find that *being with* and *being like* Jesus involves:

- Talking to Him in prayer
- Listening to Him in the Bible
- Reaching out to those He wants to touch
- Sharing your life with His other disciples
- Entrusting every area of your life to His guidance

HOW DO I USE THIS BOOK?

Each of the first four sections of this book deals with one of the four crucial dimensions of the Christian life. The main topics listed in the table of contents are from *Beating the Churchgoing Blahs* by Robert Thornton Henderson (InterVarsity). They are the same basics of the Christian life that Christ's disciples have been pursuing for centuries.

"Knowing the King" is what an old saint named Benedict called "spiritual formation"; it chiefly involves prayer and also constant dependence on God amid the trials of life. "Knowing the Faith" comes from studying the Bible and hearing it taught (Benedict's "theological formation"). The topics "Called to Be Sent" and "The Body of Christ" involve reaching outward to the unbelieving world and to Christian brothers and sisters. (Some Christians call these two areas "evangelism" and "fellowship.")

No matter which term is used, these four critical pursuits depend on each other for real fruitfulness. Your faith will be much more rich and stable if you start getting your feet wet in all of these crucial areas of the Christian life.

The fifth section of this book, "Life in the World," might be called "The Christian in Action." "Life in the World" deals with practical life issues: how being a Christian affects your ways of making decisions, your work, your relationships with people, and your use of money. You'll find that functioning as a dynamic Christian in these areas depends on the quality of your prayer life, Bible study, and relationships with believers and unbelievers. You'll also find that, far from making your life more burdened, approaching the Christian life God's way will free you from much of the anxiety that issues such as money, work, and relationships produce. We've tried to make it easy for you to find what you want to read about. You can skim the table of contents for questions that interest you.

If you are new to the Christian faith, we suggest you begin with "What does it mean to call God 'Father'?" (page 20), "What does it mean to depend on God in daily life?" (pages 65–66), "What is the gospel?" (pages 69–70), and "Who am I?" (pages 97–99). When you grasp these basics, you can approach the rest of discipleship knowing that the Father loves you and the Spirit empowers you to become what Jesus died for you to be.

KNOWING THE KING

The world becomes a strange mad, painful place, and life in it a disappointing and unpleasant business, for those who do not know about God. Disregard the study of God, and you sentence yourself to stumble and blunder through life blindfolded, as it were, with no sense of direction and no understanding of what surrounds you. This way you can waste your life and lose your soul.

J. I. PACKER, *KNOWING GOD*

DISCOVERING THE CHARACTER OF GOD

The Lᴀᴀᴀ the Lᴀᴀᴀ the compassionate and gracious God, slow to anger, abounding in love and faithfulness, maintaining love to thousands, and forgiving wickedness, rebellion and sin. Yet he does not leave the guilty unpunished.

EXODUS 34:6-7

WHO IS GOD, AND WHAT IS HE LIKE?[1]

The Bible systematically adapts human language to talk about God. It thereby gives us an adequate idea of His nature and character, even though His essence is beyond our mental capacity to grasp.

Yahweh. *YHWH* is the personal name God used when He made His covenant with Israel (Exodus 3:14-15). It means "I Aᴀ Wᴭᴀ I Aᴀ" or "I Wᴭᴀᴀ BᲩ Wᴭᴀᴀ I Wᴭᴀᴀ BᲩ." That is, God *exists* ultimately and independently and is *actively present* with His people.

Because the Jews eventually decided that God's name was too holy to be spoken, they began to call Him "the Lord" and most English translations render the name "the Lᴀᴀᴀ."

These are other Old Testament names for God:

- *Elohim*—"God," the transcendent One (Genesis 1:1)
- *El-Shaddai*—"God Almighty," the mountain One (Genesis 35:11)
- *Adonai*—"Sovereign LORD," sovereign over everything (Genesis 15:2)
- *Yahweh Sabaoth*—"the LORD of hosts" (NASB) or "the LORD Almighty" (NIV), Ruler of the armies of heaven (Psalm 24:10)
- *Qadosh Yisrael*—the "Holy One of Israel" (Psalm 71:22)

The Trinity. God is as truly three Persons as He is One. (See, for instance, John 14–16; 1 Corinthians 12:3-6; 2 Corinthians 13:14.) It is a mystery to us how this is possible, because we don't know any other beings that are three distinct persons while remaining one being. But the biblical writers insist that the Father is fully God, Jesus is fully God, the Holy Spirit is fully God. They are not the same Persons, and there is only one God.

God's attributes.

Self-existent. God can't stop existing. He is the only Being that has life in and of Himself (John 5:26).

Personal. God has personality, consciousness, choice, and life. We relate to Him as a person, not as a force (Acts 17:27).

Simple, perfect, unchanging. God never experiences conflict within Himself. He is entirely involved in everything He is and does. His nature and ways never change, and they couldn't improve. His changelessness is not that "of an eternally frozen pose, but the moral consistency that holds him to his own principles of action and leads him to deal differently with those who change their own behavior towards him"[2] (Numbers 23:19; James 1:17).

Infinite, bodiless, omnipresent, eternal. God is not bound by space or time. He is Spirit. He is present everywhere. He is always aware of everything past, present, and future (John 4:24).

Purposeful, all-powerful, sovereign. God has a plan for the universe. He works with and through His creatures to accomplish His purpose (1) without violating human freedom of choice or the nature of what He has made and (2) despite human and satanic opposition (Luke 1:37).

Transcendent, immanent. God is distinct from His creation, does not need it, and is beyond the grasp of any created intellect. Yet, "he permeates the world in sustaining creative power, shaping and steering it in a way that keeps it on its planned course"[3] (Isaiah 55:8-9; 57:15).

Impassible (not "impassive, unfeeling"). No created being can inflict pain on God against His will. Amazingly, He chooses to feel grief, anger, and compassion because of us. He chose to suffer horribly at the Crucifixion. Otherwise, His joy and delight are boundless and constant (Isaiah 63:9; Philippians 2:6-8).

God's character.

Perfect love. Love is giving at one's own cost for the recipient's benefit. The supreme example of love is that God the Father gave His Son to suffer so that humans could be freed from condemnation. God is never selfish or cruel, even though we often don't understand why He does things. God isn't just loving toward us; He is love in His essence. The Persons of the Trinity are constantly exulting in and acting out Their love for each other (1 John 4:7-9).

Perfect wisdom. God not only has the power to govern the universe and the love to desire the best for His subjects, but He also has the wisdom to figure out how to achieve His greatest glory and His subjects' highest good. He always knows what He is doing, even when we don't (Romans 11:33).

Holiness. God's love is not blind indulgence. He detests evil and must show His just anger against it. His holiness demanded that a price be paid for human rebellion; His love determined that He would pay the price Himself. His love desires that we be intimate with Him; His holiness requires that we be made righteous for this to occur (Revelation 15:4).

Moral perfection. God is utterly truthful, faithful, merciful, generous, patient, just, and good. This is how He deals with everyone, even rebels (Psalm 103:1-18; Hebrews 6:18).

WHAT DOES IT MEAN TO CALL GOD "FATHER"?

When we commit ourselves to Jesus as Lord and Savior, we are reborn. Jesus' Father becomes our Father by adoption and new spiritual "genetics." We have the right to call Him "Abba" (Romans 8:15), which means "Papa," a respectful but intimately affectionate name. We can go to Him with all our concerns, receive from Him all the love and sense of importance we need, and confidently confess our sins to Him. He is everything a Father should be (Matthew 7:9-11; Luke 15:11-32; Hebrews 12:4-11).

WHO IS JESUS?

Fully God. Jesus participated in creating the universe and continues to partake in keeping it on course. He is the exact expression of the Father's moral character and personality (John 1:1-2; Colossians 1:15-20; Hebrews 1:3). Every attribute and trait of God listed earlier is true of Jesus. When He came to earth, He voluntarily and temporarily gave up His infinity, omnipresence, and so on. The humility of this sacrifice was awesome.

Fully human. Jesus took on every physical, emotional, and mental human trait, but His body, mind, will, and emotions were not corrupted by sin. Having emptied Himself of His divine rights, He worked His miracles by the power of the Holy Spirit, not by His power as the Son of God (Matthew 12:28). He resisted Satan by the strength of the Spirit and the commitment of His human will. He suffered what we suffer and used only the power that is available to us so that He could understand and help us in our temptations. As Scripture tells us, "We have one [a high priest] who has been tempted in every way, just as we are—yet was without sin" (Hebrews 4:15). "Because he himself suffered when he was tempted, he is able to help those who are being tempted" (Hebrews 2:18).

After His resurrection, Jesus did not discard His humanity. For all eternity, He bears in His glorified body the scars of crucifixion, the marks of a love so incredible that it must leave even the angels speechless.

Names of Jesus.

Christ. "The Anointed One," the Jewish title of the nation's greatest King, a descendant of David. Christus is a Greek translation of the Hebrew word *Meshiach,* "Messiah" (Luke 9:20).

Jesus. "The Lord saves" (Matthew 1:21).

Immanuel. "God with us" (Matthew 1:23).

Lord. Sovereign over everything, under the Father (Acts 2:36; 1 Corinthians 15:24-28).

Wonderful Counselor, Mighty God, Everlasting Father, Prince of Peace (Isaiah 9:6).

Son of God (Mark 1:1).

Son of Man. Jesus called Himself this (Mark 2:28). He was a man, yet the glorious One foretold in Daniel 7:13-14.

WHO IS THE HOLY SPIRIT, AND WHAT DOES HE DO?

The Holy Spirit is the third Person of the Trinity. He is thus fully God and a person, not a force.

The *ruach* (breath, wind, spirit) of God appears in the Old Testament as God's energy let loose. The New Testament adds that the Spirit is a person distinct from the Father and the Son. During Jesus' life on earth, He was His disciples' ally, advocate, counselor, strengthener, and supporter. When Jesus returned to the Father, He sent the Spirit to fill those roles (John 14:16).

The Spirit:

- Shares in creation (Genesis 1:2)
- Reveals God's messages, and thereby teaches how to live fruitfully
- Enables faith, repentance, obedience, praise, prayer, strong and wise leadership, and skill for creative work
- Reveals to us who Jesus is and what He wants us to know
- Convicts believers and unbelievers of guilt

- Unites us to Jesus in rebirth so that we are the limbs of His body and sharers in His kingdom
- Assures believers that we are God's children and heirs
- Mediates our intimate sharing with the Father and Son, our first installment and guarantee of heaven's life
- Transforms us "progressively through prayer and conflict with sin into Christ's moral and spiritual likeness"—He gives us the power to love, to have joy and peace, and so on (Galatians 5:22-23)
- Gives gifts (abilities to witness and serve) to build up Christ's body
- Prays in and for us when we feel unable
- Enables us to know what to say when others ask about Christ
- Enables missionary action, pastoral decisions, and leadership[4] (John 14:15-27; 15:26–16:16; 20:19-23; Romans 8:1-27; 1 Corinthians 12:1–14:40)

WHAT ARE THE GIFTS OF THE SPIRIT?

The gifts of the Spirit are abilities given by the Holy Spirit that equip us to serve Christ and build up His body. They are distinct from "the fruit of the Spirit" (Galatians 5:22-23), which are Christian character qualities. Romans 12:3-8 and 1 Corinthians 12:8-10,28 list some of the gifts the Spirit gives. From 1 Corinthians 12–14 and elsewhere, we learn the following:

The purpose of all gifts is to build up the body. Gifts are not given for fame, recognition, or self-fulfillment. They "are not our property to use as we please; they are a trust committed to us by

God to use for others and for His glory as He directs"[5] (1 Peter 4:10-11).

Gifts are not merit badges or rewards. All gifts are given by grace, undeserved. Publicly known or highly gifted people are not necessarily more holy or worthy than those who have humble, hidden gifts.

All gifts are essential to God's purposes. You should never feel unimportant or more important than someone else. Don't be wrapped up in (or put down by someone else who is wrapped up in) spiritual status-seeking.

Every Christian has at least one gift. To say you have no gift is to say you have no function in the body.

The Spirit of God bestows gifts sovereignly. He, not you, decides what your function in the body is and how gifted you will be. You can trust His decision to be perfectly wise and good for the body as a whole, even if you would like a flashier gift for your own satisfaction or pride.

Gifts must be developed and exercised. You get a gift by grace, but it takes hard work and time — study and practice — to learn to use it. God holds us responsible for how we develop what He has given.

The effective use of every gift is dependent on faith in Christ. It is not enough to acknowledge that the gift is sovereignly given and to use it. We must constantly and consciously depend on Christ for His enabling power. We have to avoid taking God for granted either by not using the gift or by not relying on His power.

The effective use of gifts requires participation in a local body. Gifts are meant to concretely build up the body. The only way to build up the church universal is to commit yourself and contribute to a specific body of believers.

Gifts are useless, even harmful, without love. Unless love permeates all our relationships, we will destroy the unity that the gifts are supposed to build.

HOW CAN I DISCOVER MY GIFTS?

Commitment. If you are committed to do what God wants you to do, He will reveal His gifts to you.

Experience. What has and hasn't God given you to do? In what service has God blessed your efforts, and in what areas has He not? What opportunities for service have and haven't been open to you? Through past experience God shows us the areas where we can serve Him best.

Natural abilities and temperament. Spiritual gifts aren't the same as natural abilities, but they often build on or are consistent with natural inclinations. A teacher may be a naturally good student supernaturally gifted to pass on what he learns.

On the other hand, God may call and gift you for a function that leaves dormant some of your natural abilities and that challenges your temperament. For instance, God might call a shy musician or scientist to a public ministry alongside or even instead of her other work.

Other Christians' confirmations. God can use other Christians to give us guidance in discovering our spiritual gifts. In what areas do others say you have helped them? What do mature Christians say when you ask for their input regarding your gifts?

HOW CAN I CORRECTLY USE MY GIFTS?

Ask yourself the following questions:

- The Holy Spirit represents Christ. So, is my use of this gift misrepresenting, displacing, or dishonoring Christ (1 John 4:1-6)?
- The Holy Spirit will not contradict what He said to the apostles and prophets who wrote the Bible. Does my use of this gift undermine the authority or teaching of the Bible?
- Does exercising this gift tear down the body? Does it cause dissension or other harm?
- Am I using this gift in any way other than in love?

WHAT DOES IT MEAN TO BE FILLED WITH THE SPIRIT?

To be filled with the Holy Spirit means to be under the Spirit's control. In his gospel and in Acts, Luke used the word *filled* (*full, filling,* and so on) in the following ways:

- "When people are given an initial endowment of the Spirit to fit them for God's service"
- "When they are inspired to make important utterances"
- For "the continuous process of being filled with the Spirit or the corresponding state of being full"

So, "a person already filled with the Spirit can receive a fresh filling for a specific task, or a continuous filling."[6]

Paul exhorted us to be filled with the Spirit (Ephesians 5:18). We do this by:

- Constantly asking God for His presence and power
- Daily spending time in God's presence in worship
- Continually resisting the desires of our sinful nature, so that the Spirit is free to act

WHAT DOES IT MEAN TO BE BAPTIZED WITH THE SPIRIT?

Being baptized with the Spirit is the same as the initial filling described earlier (Acts 1:5; 2:4). It happens when we commit our lives to Christ and yield control of our lives to His Spirit. The recurring experience is always called filling, not baptism. In one sense, we are individually immersed into God's Spirit so that He becomes the controlling influence of our lives. In another sense, we are "all baptized by one Spirit into one body" (1 Corinthians 12:13) so that He immerses and unites us into Christ and with each other. This baptism is the end of rugged individualism and self-reliance; we are ruled by God's Spirit and devoted to other Christians.

HOW CAN A LOVING GOD SEND PEOPLE TO HELL?

God made many objects and living creatures that He loves and enjoys, but they have no capacity to love Him back. Stars, rocks, trees, and animals are all like this. But God also chose to make some creatures with the capacity to love, feel, reason, and make moral choices. He wanted to have personal relationships with beings He made, the kind of relationships that requires all these capacities.

God also wanted to demonstrate the magnitude of His love, the extent to which He would go for the well-being of His creatures. Above all, He wanted to display to all His living creatures His glory, the majesty and attributes that make Him alone worthy of worship. Having created beings able to choose to love and worship Him, He wanted to fully exhibit why they should do so.

With these goals in mind, God created humans. The first humans chose against God and doomed their descendants to do the same unless God intervened. This God did by sending His Son—God in human flesh—to suffer temptation, separation from the Father, and death. God ordained which men and women would respond to this unthinkable act of love, yet mysteriously, each person's freedom to choose is real.

The choice is all-important. In *The Great Divorce*, C. S. Lewis described inhabitants of hell who took a bus tour to visit heaven. They hated it. They found it boring and uncomfortable. As miserable as they were in hell, it was the home where they fit. God had made them or they had made themselves (the two are the same), unable to enjoy the eternal presence of God.

In *Mere Christianity*, Lewis described how a person becomes a citizen of hell:

> People often think of Christian morality as a kind of bargain in which God says, "If you keep a lot of rules I'll reward you, and if you don't I'll do the other thing." I do not think that is the best way of looking at it. I would much rather say that every time you make a choice you are turning the central part of you, the part of you that chooses, into something a little different from

what it was before. And taking your life as a whole, with all your innumerable choices, all your life long you are slowly turning this central thing either into a heavenly creature or a hellish creature: either into a creature that is in harmony with God, and with other creatures, and with itself, or else into one that is in a state of war and hatred with God, and with its fellow-creatures, and with itself. To be the one kind of creature is heaven: that is, it is joy and peace and knowledge and power. To be the other means madness, horror, idiocy, rage, impotence, and eternal loneliness. Each of us at each moment is progressing to the one state or the other.[7]

WHAT CAN I EXPECT OR TRUST GOD TO DO FOR ME?

You can expect God to meet your deepest needs in limited measure while you are alive. He will:

- Provide food, clothing, and shelter, and protect you from physical death, until He judges it time to bring you home to Him
- Nurture you with the unconditional love you crave (if you let Him)
- Give you a task that is eternally important and empower you with the ability to do it
- Send the partners you need to share in this work
- Furnish all the guidance you need (if you are willing to listen)

- Supply all the trying people and circumstances—all the suffering—you need to grow into the likeness of Christ
- Raise you, soul and body, after death to reign with Him eternally in joy, reveling in His love—at that time your need for love and significance will be fully met, and you will lack nothing

You can't expect God to:

- Give you everything you want (or think you need)
- Protect you from pain
- See to it that people love and respect you
- Make you materially rich
- Make all your decisions for you
- Make you as happy as you will be in the next life

LEARNING ABOUT PRAYER

Don't worry about anything; instead, pray about everything.
Tell God what you need, and thank him for all he has done.

PHILIPPIANS 4:6, NLT

WHAT IS PRAYER?

Prayer is conversing with God—talking to Him, listening to Him, being in His presence. Prayer includes sharing your thoughts, feelings, doubts, problems, complaints, hopes, and joys. It involves confessing sin, worshipping God, committing yourself to obey Him, giving thanks, making requests for yourself and others, and just being available to God.

WHY SHOULD I PRAY?

When you love someone, you want to be with that person. You want to share your thoughts and enjoy the other person's presence. Prayer is the way we spend time with our Beloved and become intimate with Him.

> I belong to my lover,
>> and his desire is for me. (Song of Songs 7:10)

As God is our Beloved, so also He is our Lord. Prayer is one of the ways we train our will to serve Him—adoring His greatness, acknowledging our weakness, acquiring His perspective, and seeking His specific instructions. Prayer and Bible study work together to immerse us in our Lord's attitudes, values, desires, methods, and goals. If we want to obey Him, we need to spend time with Him.

Finally, God is our Father (Romans 8:15). Instead of making robots that would do His will automatically, He created humans who could become sons and daughters. Whether we are spiritual infants or adults, we all have needs, feelings, and responsibilities. Our Father nurtures and disciplines us whether we ask Him to or not, for He knows our needs. But, like a human father, He likes His children to tell Him what they wish for, what they are feeling, and how much they appreciate their Father.

WHAT ARE THANKSGIVING, PRAISE, AND WORSHIP?

The Bible does not make strict distinctions between thanksgiving, praise, and worship, so Christians have developed a variety of helpful understandings. Here are some helpful insights:

> Worship begins with praise. Praise is simply the act of complimenting or acknowledging the goodness of a person or thing. . . . We praise athletes, beautiful women, wine, food, and so on. Praise, as the act of complimenting, can be applied both to things and to God. Worship, by contrast, applies only to that which is divine and it occurs on an entirely different spiritual plane.

Praise is a human activity which acknowledges God. Worship is God's activity in us in response to praise as He catches us up to Himself in loving embrace. Worship is fraught with the wonder of an intimacy in which God has taken the initiative. In worship we move past what we are doing as human beings and we become lost in what He is doing in and through us. Praise prepares us, but no more than that. . . .

Of the many Old Testament Hebrew words for "worship," *shachah* is a common one. It means to "*bow the self down.*" God increases; I decrease. I am awed by Him. My self dies, and with it my honor, my dignity, my pride [Exodus 34:5-9; Joshua 5:13-15].[1]

Some Christians view all of life as worship as we "do it all in the name of the Lord Jesus" (Colossians 3:17), offering our "bodies as living sacrifices . . . this is [our] spiritual act of worship" (Romans 12:1). Others view work and service as the outflow of worship and something to be offered to God in worship.[2] Praise, in either of these views, is an aspect of worship by which we celebrate who God is and what He has done.

WHY SHOULD I PRAISE GOD? IS HE AN EGOTIST?

Through praise you escape self-centeredness. God does not emphasize praise, thanksgiving, and worship "because He is an egotist with selfish desires, but because He has our best interests at heart. Praise and thanksgiving help us rise above self-centeredness to Christ-centeredness. They focus our hearts and minds on the Lord and make us more like Him. We cheat ourselves when we neglect them, for they are a tonic that promotes joy and spiritual vigor."[3]

You grow in faith and experience God's power. Praising and worshipping God strengthen our faith, because we focus on what we *know* is true about Him instead of focusing on what we *feel* about our circumstances. Praise and worship release God to act in power. When faced with disaster, King Jehoshaphat praised God for six long verses (2 Chronicles 20:6-11):

> O LORD, God of our fathers, are you not the God who is in heaven? You rule over all the kingdoms of the nations. Power and might are in your hand, and no one can withstand you. (verse 6)

Then, in verse 12, Jehoshaphat stated his distress. When the Lord's answer came, Jehoshaphat and all the people responded:

> Jehoshaphat bowed with his face to the ground, and all the people of Judah and Jerusalem fell down in worship before the LORD. Then some Levites . . . stood up and praised the LORD, the God of Israel, with a very loud voice. (2 Chronicles 20:18-19)

The nation's victory over its attackers was astounding.

You experience God's presence. In *Reflections on the Psalms*, C. S. Lewis described a time when he struggled with why praise was important: "I did not see that it is in the process of being worshipped that God communicates His presence to men. It is not of course the only way. But for many people at many times the 'fair beauty of the Lord' is revealed chiefly or only while they worship Him together."[4]

God deserves it. Furthermore, we praise God because He deserves it. We owe Him everything, so we would be less than human if we didn't overflow with gratitude and love.

> I will exalt you, O LORD,
>> for you lifted me out of the depths. (Psalm 30:1)

> You are worthy, our Lord and God,
>> to receive glory and honor and power,
> for you created all things,
>> and by your will they were created
>> and have their being. (Revelation 4:11)

You will enjoy it. Finally, praise and worship are pleasures for us. C. S. Lewis wrote,

> I think we delight to praise what we enjoy because the praise not merely expresses but completes the enjoyment; it is its appointed consummation. It is not out of compliment that lovers keep on telling one another how beautiful they are; the delight is incomplete till it is expressed. . . . The worthier the object, the more intense this delight would be. If it were possible for a created soul fully . . . to "appreciate," that is to love and delight in, the worthiest object of all, and simultaneously at every moment to give this delight perfect expression, then that soul would be in supreme beatitude.[5]

Read some of the praise psalms aloud (for instance: 8; 19; 29; 30; 33; 47; 66; 100; 103–108; 111; 113; 136; 138; 145–150). Or read aloud some of the praise songs from Revelation (4:8,11; 5:9-10,12-13; 7:12; 11:15-18; 15:3-4; 19:18). Notice how the writers express their feelings about God, and pay attention to the kinds of things they praise Him for. Then take time to tell God what you appreciate about Him. Let praise bring you to the point when you spiritually (perhaps even physically) bow down and worship the Lord.

WHAT ARE SOME FALSE IDEAS ABOUT PRAISE, AND HOW CAN I AVOID THEIR PITFALLS?

False ideas about praise can cause problems:

If we view praise as a cure for every ailment and the primary secret of success in the Christian life, we are likely to neglect other essentials—prayer for ourselves and others, diligent intake of God's Word, and daily obedience to Christ as Lord. If we place too much emphasis on the emotional aspects of praise, we become disillusioned when we reach one of life's emotionally dry periods. Or we discourage sincere believers who seldom experience strong emotions as they praise, making them think they will never be able to develop an acceptable praise life. Yet if we fear and avoid emotions in our praise, we miss much of the enjoyment and many of the benefits that can be ours.[6]

To avoid these pitfalls, remember the following principles:

Focus on facts, not feelings. Focus on what you know is true about God, yourself, and the world. Build your praise on God's Word, and live by your will and God's grace rather than your feelings. Praising God will often lift your emotions as it strengthens your faith and brings you into God's presence, but don't do it for an emotional high.

Don't pretend you feel wonderful about God when you don't. You can choose to worship as an act of your will while acknowledging to God and others that you feel sad, anxious, doubtful, or angry. Acknowledge your feelings; just don't let them rule you.

Don't use praise to try to manipulate God into doing what you want. This never works, as God knows your heart.

Don't use praise as a substitute for seeking intelligent solutions for life's problems.

WHY SHOULD I CONFESS MY SINS TO GOD? DOESN'T HE ALREADY KNOW THEM?

Psalm 32:3-5; 51:1-7; and 1 John 1:8-9 illustrate the following purposes of confession:

Hidden sin festers and corrupts, divides, and destroys. God knows your sin, but until you acknowledge it, you can convince yourself that it isn't really sin, that you don't have to do anything about it, and that it hasn't done any harm. Confession is the first step toward repentance, turning around and stopping the wrong action or attitude.

Confession releases forgiveness. If you aren't guilty, the blood of Christ can do nothing for you. If you acknowledge that you are guilty, then God can cleanse you.

Confession brings you into reality. God wants your relationship with Him to be based on truth, on reality. *Confess* comes from a Latin verb meaning "to say the same as." Agreeing with God about what is true founds your relationship on reality. Confession frees you from the bondage of lies, self-deceit, and delusion that Satan wants to keep you in.

Confession restores your relationship with God. If you live in falsehood and unforgiveness, it is impossible for God to hear and answer your prayers (Isaiah 59:1-2).

Confession makes life more pleasant. Not confessing robs your joy, your peace, your comfort around God, and ultimately even your health. It's not worth it!

HOW SHOULD I CONFESS?

Psalm 51 is an excellent model for confession. You will sometimes need to confess specific sins you have committed, while at other times you simply want to acknowledge your frailty before the Lord.

An important feature of confession is telling God how you feel about things. The Psalms are full of what we might call "negative confession," in which the psalmist told God how he felt, how disappointed he was in God, and so on.

I am feeble and utterly crushed;

I groan in anguish of heart. (Psalm 38:8)

Negative confessions were not expressions of self-pity but honesty. In Psalm 38 and elsewhere, David interspersed frankness with decisions to trust despite his feelings and with petitions to the God he trusted.

> All my longings lie open before you, O Lord;
>> my sighing is not hidden from you.
> My heart pounds, my strength fails me;
>> even the light has gone from my eyes.
> My friends and companions avoid me because of my wounds;
>> my neighbors stay far away. . . .
> I am like a deaf man, who cannot hear,
>> like a mute, who cannot open his mouth. . . .
> I wait for you, O Lord;
>> you will answer, O Lord my God. . . .
> I confess my iniquity;
>> I am troubled by my sin. . . .
> O Lord, do not forsake me;
>> be not far from me, O my God.
> Come quickly to help me,
>> O Lord my Savior. (Psalm 38:9-11,13,15,18,21-22)

Confessing his feelings and his sinful attitudes helped David let go of them and make the decision to rely on God.

Here are two warnings to remember in confession:

Don't manufacture guilt.

Often, to be sure, there is something definite for which to ask for forgiveness. This is a plain sailing. But, like you, I often find one or other of two less manageable states: either a vague feeling of guilt or a sly, and equally vague, self-approval. What are we to do with these? . . .

I have, on the whole, come to the conclusion that one can't directly do anything about either feeling. One is not to believe either—indeed, how can one believe a fog? I come back to St. John: "if our heart condemn us, God is greater than our heart" [1 John 3:20, KJV]. And equally, if our heart flatter us, God is greater than our heart. . . .

If I am right, the conclusion is that when our conscience won't come down to brass-tacks but will only vaguely accuse or vaguely approve, we must say to it, like Herbert, "Peace prattler"—and get on.[7]

Don't let confession be a substitute for repentance. Remorse (feelings and words) is not repentance (actions).

WHAT IS THE POINT OF PETITIONARY PRAYER IF GOD KNOWS WHAT I NEED BETTER THAN I DO?

Petition in prayer is simply asking God for what we want. Because God knows us completely, including our needs and our desires, petition may seem an unnecessary exercise. But in unveiling our desires voluntarily, we act toward God as persons, rather than as things. Likewise, we treat Him as a Father, a Lover, a Friend, rather than as the far-off all-knowing machine that turns the universe.

The point of petition (and intercession) is not to change God's mind, to get Him to do something good that He wouldn't do unless we twisted His arm. God doesn't live in our time frame. He doesn't suddenly rearrange everything in response to a petition. He lives in eternity, seeing the whole of time at a glance. From the foundation of the world, He sees every prayer and takes/took each one into account as He plans/planned what would happen. We don't pray to change God's mind, but (through the mystery of a love relationship with the Almighty) to be "taken into account."[8]

WHAT ATTITUDES SHOULD SHAPE MY PETITIONS?
Have faith that God is powerful and loving enough to act.

Which of you, if his son asks for bread, will give him a stone? Or if he asks for a fish, will give him a snake? If you, then, though you are evil, know how to give good gifts to your children, how much more will your Father in heaven give good gifts to those who ask him! (Matthew 7:9-11)

See also Mark 1:40-42; 9:22-24.
Don't try to manufacture faith.

The state of mind which desperate desire working on a strong imagination can manufacture is not faith in the Christian sense. It is a feat of psychological gymnastics.[9]

God promises that if we have genuine certainty that something is His will in a particular instance, then we can pray for it with confidence (Mark 11:24). However, such faith depends on walking with God in maturity and on a special insight from God about the particular situation. We are welcome and encouraged to ask for things without this absolute faith, with only faith in God's character and His general will. "Yes" answers to such prayers are not guaranteed, but answers are. "Help me overcome my unbelief!" (Mark 9:24) is a legitimate, honest prayer.

Being heard is more important than getting what you ask. The Bible speaks much less about getting results from prayer than about being "heard" or "answered." False religion is result-oriented; Christian prayer is relationship-oriented. "We can bear to be refused but not to be ignored."[10]

Accept "later," "no," and silence as answers. Jesus asked His Father to release Him from having to be crucified. Hebrews 5:7 says, "He offered up prayers and petitions with loud cries and tears to the one who could save him from death, and he was heard because of his reverent submission." Jesus was heard, but the answer was no (to escaping crucifixion) and yes (to ultimate deliverance from death).

We need to know that God knows what is best for us and others. He won't give us a stone if we ask for bread, nor will He give us a stone if we ask for a stone.

Persevere. When we persevere in prayer we are demonstrating that we have placed all our hope in God and that we trust Him despite outward appearances that tempt us to despair.

Jesus told outrageous parables to spur His disciples to persevere in prayer. One parable concerned a man who gave his neighbor bread only because the neighbor kept on bothering him (Luke 11:5-8). Another was about a judge who gave a woman justice only because he was sick of listening to the woman's pleas (Luke 18:1-8). If even such people respond to persistence, won't a loving Father God?

Pray with a confidence that is based on what Jesus has done for you (Romans 5:1; Hebrews 4:16). Because Jesus paid the penalty for our sins on the cross, we have been restored to relationship with the Father. We have "confidence," a legal right to approach the King with our requests.

Pray in Jesus' name (John 16:23). We have access to the King because we know the King's Son. Praying in His name means saying to the Father, "Jesus said I could ask You this on His authority." If what we are asking for is consistent with Jesus' character, methods, and goals, then we can have utter confidence that we will be heard if we pray under Jesus' authority. If not, we can expect the Father to answer, "Jesus would never have authorized such a request!"

Pray in accord with God's will (1 John 5:14-15). The best way to learn what God's will is and what you can legitimately ask in Jesus' name is to study the Bible. God's specific will for a situation will never contradict His general will as revealed in the whole of Scripture.

Let your prayers flow from a life rooted in Christ (John 15:7). If we are remaining or abiding in Christ, like branches in a vine, gaining our nourishment from Him, seeking to do His will, and quickly confessing any sins that block our relationship, then we will know what God wants us to pray, and we can be confident of answers.

Tell God what you want. Honesty is crucial. God is interested in the large prayers for nations and the tiny prayers for your pleasure. He cares about your personal, physical desires as well as your spiritual needs. If you tell Him, "Father, I know this is trivial, but I can't stop thinking about it, and I really want . . ." then God will decide whether to grant your desire or help you let go of it. Suppressing the distraction only makes it worse. If you ask for something you shouldn't, then God will either lovingly give it to you to teach you something, or He won't. He is bigger than your mistakes.

Don't make demands. Confidence to make humble, trusting requests of a loving Father is not the same as arrogance to make demands. It's worth checking every now and then to see whether you are seeking to claim promises with an attitude that shows you have forgotten who is the center of the universe or that suggests you know what is best better than He does.

Don't pray for something if you aren't willing to do what God may tell you to do. Jesus taught His disciples to pray, "Your kingdom come, your will be done on earth as it is in heaven" (Matthew 6:10). If you pray, "Your will be done," you are volunteering to do His will.

WHAT IS THE PURPOSE OF INTERCESSION?

My command is this: Love each other as I have loved you. Greater love has no one than this, that he lay down his life for his friends. (John 15:12-13)

> Carry each other's burdens, and in this way you will fulfill the
> law of Christ. (Galatians 6:2)

To intercede is to stand between, to mediate, to make requests on another's behalf. Jesus' work of redemption is forever finished, but His work of intercession for us goes on continually (Hebrews 7:25). Likewise, one of the ways we love others as He loves us is by interceding for them, carrying their burdens to God in prayer.

True intercession begins with God. God's Spirit moves in your heart to invite God to set things straight (Romans 8:26). Intercession is necessary because, although God is sovereign, He has given us free will. He wants sons and daughters, not robots. God doesn't need us to help Him run the world, but in His omnipotent wisdom He plans to prepare us to reign with Him (Revelation 5:9-10). To do this, He delegates to His servants the authority to invite Him to act. When we intercede, we shouldn't be trying to change His mind but inviting Him to do His will.

God told Ezekiel that He was going to have to destroy Jerusalem because:

> I looked for a man among them who would build up the wall
> and stand before me in the gap on behalf of the land so I would
> not have to destroy it, but I found none. (Ezekiel 22:30)

This is the intercessor's job: to stand between a person and God and beg blessing rather than curse for him, and to carry to Christ the griefs and burdens that are too heavy for a person to bear. (For more examples of intercession, see Genesis 18:16-33;

Exodus 32:9-14,30-34; Psalm 106:23; Daniel 9:4-19; John 17:1-26; Ephesians 1:15-23; 3:14-21; Philippians 1:9-11; Colossians 1:9-14.)

WHEN AND HOW SHOULD I INTERCEDE?

When you sense a need in your heart, pray. Open your eyes and heart to the needs of people around you. Love gives and forgets self. Focus on others' needs, and make them your own.

When you feel impotent, pray. The man in Luke 11:5-8 had no bread for his guest, so he went to a friend who did have bread. Cultivate the sense that God's power is made perfect in your weakness (2 Corinthians 12:9). When there is nothing you can do but pray, it is the most important thing you can do.

Don't let prayer be a substitute for action.

I'm afraid, however, I detect two much less attractive reasons for the ease of my own intercessory prayers. One is that I am often, I believe, praying for others when I should be doing things for them. It's so much easier to pray for a bore than to go and see him. And the other is like unto it. Suppose I pray that you may be given grace to withstand your besetting sin. . . . Well, all the work has to be done by God and you. If I pray against my own besetting sin there will be work for me.[11]

Pray in unity with others.

If two of you on earth agree about anything you ask for, it will be done for you by my Father in heaven. For where two or

three come together in my name, there am I with them.
(Matthew 18:19-20)

Coming together in Jesus' name and agreeing is not just a matter of sitting in the same room and saying "Amen" together. It means that a group of Christians is united in purpose, committed to each other's highest good, acting together, and cleansed of any unforgiveness among them.

Have faith that God hears and answers prayer.

Persist and persevere.

Pray according to Christ's will, character, and authority.

WHAT IS CHRISTIAN MEDITATION? HOW DO I PRACTICE IT?

The meditation practiced in Eastern religions is a matter of emptying your mind and opening yourself up spiritually to whatever voice or influence happens by. Christian meditation aims to focus your mind in openness to God's voice, and no other.

Christian meditation is the discipline of focusing your heart on what you already have in Christ. When you became a Christian, all of Christ came to dwell in you, all of the Holy Spirit, and all of the Father. Everything you need to enable you to think and act like Christ in all situations is in your heart, where Christ lives (2 Peter 1:3-4).

In biblical thought, the heart is the core of a person, the wellspring of his or her assumptions, motivations, emotions, and will. You can study the Bible and memorize volumes of facts about God and your life in Christ, but if they never sink from your head into your heart, they won't influence your habits or the way you respond in a crisis. All the power is there inside of you, and all the promises are there in the Bible, but you have to do something to lay hold of them in your heart.

Jesus was able to walk through seething crowds (Luke 4:28-30), and the apostles were able to humbly resist threats of death (Acts 4:1-31), because they knew in the core of themselves who they were and who God was. This kind of inner-rooted knowledge leads to peace and is the fruit of meditating on God and His Word.

> I have hidden your word in my heart
>> that I might not sin against you. . . .
> Oh, how I love your law!
>> I meditate on it all day long. . . .
> My eyes stay open through the watches of the night,
>> that I may meditate on your promises. (Psalm 119:11,97,148)

Christians use the word *meditation* to describe two slightly different things. The first is a directed, focused thinking in which you mull over a passage of Scripture to draw out its meat. The second is a kind of prayer. It is related to meditating on Scripture in that it is intended to quiet your brain enough to let God's Word sink into your heart.

> In your anger do not sin;
>> when you are on your beds,
>> search your hearts and be silent. (Psalm 4:4)

Be still, and know that I am God. (Psalm 46:10)

The words *still* and *silent* here mean "to let go," "to cease," "to stand still." When angry (or anxious, or upset, or uncertain), God doesn't want us to suppress our emotions. That makes us outwardly silent but not inwardly still. Instead, He wants us to search our hearts ("commune" in the KJV), expose them to His gaze, and let what He has to say transform us. The following is a way of doing this, which you can call "meditation" or "becoming still before God." It uses the pattern of the Psalms.

Confess and release fears, tensions, and distractions. Getting rid of distractions is tough. The harder you try not to think about your pressing deadline or your sore neck, the more likely these are to whirl and sweep you downstream. That is why many of the psalmists began by confessing their distracting feelings and concerns to the Lord (Psalm 10:1-11; 22:1-2,6-8,12-18; 42:1-5; 63:1; 73:2-14; 74:1-8; 102:3-11).

It may take five minutes or half an hour to confess and let go of your distractions. You may spend several prayer sessions before you get to the point where the distractions are stilled enough to go any further. If you find it hard to concentrate during prayer, practice disciplining your mind to focus on God during the entire day.

Focus on who God is. After confessing their feelings, the psalmists moved to confessing what they knew to be true about God. This took the form of praise tailored to the specific feelings that had been plaguing them (Psalm 22:23; 42:5-11). As you affirm the truth that applies to and quiets your feelings, sink into God's presence. Let praise draw you into worship.

Open your heart, go spiritually to the place where the Spirit of God dwells inside you, and drink of Him there.

> Jesus stood and said in a loud voice, "If anyone is thirsty, let him come to me and drink. Whoever believes in me, as the Scripture has said, streams of living water will flow from within him." By this he meant the Spirit. (John 7:37-39)

Observe in Psalm 63 the sequence of confessing feelings, entering God's presence with praise that affirms the truth about Him, and feasting on His presence:

> O God, You are my God; I shall seek You earnestly;
> My soul thirsts for You, my flesh yearns for You,
> In a dry and weary land where there is no water.
> Thus I have seen You in the sanctuary,
> To see Your power and Your glory.
> Because Your lovingkindness is better than life,
> My lips will praise You.
> So I will bless You as long as I live;
> I will lift up my hands in Your name.
> My soul is satisfied as with marrow and fatness,
> And my mouth offers praises with joyful lips.
> When I remember You on my bed,
> I meditate on You in the night watches. (verses 1-6, NASB)

Surrender. After confession and praise, the psalmists became able to see their situations in perspective. They and their enemies seemed small compared to God's greatness, so they trustfully surrendered to His will.

> Whom have I in heaven but you?
>> And earth has nothing I desire besides you.
> My flesh and my heart may fail,
>> but God is the strength of my heart
>> and my portion forever. (Psalm 73:25-26)

> My heart is not proud, O LORD,
>> my eyes are not haughty;
> I do not concern myself with great matters
>> or things too wonderful for me.
> But I have stilled and quieted my soul;
>> like a weaned child with its mother,
>> like a weaned child is my soul within me.
> O Israel, put your hope in the LORD
>> both now and forevermore. (Psalm 131:1-3)

Listen.

> I wait for the LORD, my soul waits,
>> and in his word I put my hope.
> My soul waits for the Lord
>> more than watchmen wait for the morning,
>> more than watchmen wait for the morning. (Psalm 130:5-6)

In 1 Kings 19:11-12, the Lord speaks not in the gale wind or in the earthquake but rather in "a gentle whisper." Confessing distractions, meditating on truths about God, and surrendering to His will should bring you to a stillness where you can listen for that gentle whisper. Take a few minutes to wait on God in silence. He may speak in Scripture references, other words, or feelings. He may be silent. Just enjoy His presence and be attentive.

HOW OFTEN SHOULD I PRAY?

Prayer should become something you depend on for survival. It is essential to growing in faith and avoiding emotional tailspins. Time with God in prayer and Bible study is how you attain nourishment, as a branch depends on a vine for life (John 15:1-7). Jesus was busy, so He knew He didn't have time *not* to pray.

WHAT SHOULD I DO IF MY PRAYER TIME SEEMS DRY?

> When prayer is dry, instead of giving way we should make a wider act of faith and carry on. We should say to God "I am worn out, I cannot pray really; accept, O Lord, this monotonous voice and these words of prayer, and help me." . . . It is the Holy Spirit who will in due time fill prayer, faithful and patient as it has been, with the meaning and the depth of a new life. When we stand before God in these moments of dejection we must use our will, we must pray from conviction if not from feeling, out of the faith we are aware of possessing, intellectually if not from a burning heart.[12]

WHAT SHOULD I DO IF I FEEL UNWORTHY TO APPROACH GOD?

Start by confessing, then boldly approach God with your petitions in the knowledge that Jesus has won you access.

> The more dejected we feel, the greater the necessity for prayer. And that is surely what John of Kronstadt felt one day when he was praying, watched by the Devil who was muttering, "You hypocrite, how dare you pray with your filthy mind, full of thoughts I read in it." He answered, "It is just because my mind is full of thoughts I dislike and fight that I am praying to God."[13]

HAVING AN EFFECTIVE QUIET TIME

Open my eyes that I may see wonderful things in your law.

PSALM 119:18

WHAT IS A QUIET TIME?

Quiet time is the name many Christians give to their daily time of talking and listening to God. It is also called personal devotions, an appointment with God, and so on. Having a quiet time with God each day is crucial to:

- Getting direction from God
- Growing in love for and personal knowledge of God
- Becoming more like God

The two main elements of a quiet time are prayer and Bible reading.

WHAT SHOULD I DO IN MY QUIET TIME?
Start with the proper attitudes.

Expect to be enriched by your time with the King of the universe, your loving Father.

Go reverently into His presence. Don't rush in; take time to get quiet.

Be alert. Get fully awake first. Make it a priority to get enough sleep so that you can concentrate.

Be committed to obey what you hear God saying, no matter what.

Choose a place where you can be alone. Find a place where you can concentrate on and listen to God.

Choose a time when you can be alert. First thing in the morning is a great time because it lets your quiet time set the tone for the rest of the day. However, if you are half asleep or frantic in the morning but relaxed and alert in the evening or at noon, have your time with God then. Make a commitment with God that for the next six weeks nothing will take priority over Him during the time you have set.

Commit yourself to go to bed at whatever time is necessary for you to be rested enough to be alert for God. If you have determined that time with God takes priority over time with friends or television or the Internet, then this will be possible.

Set an amount of time you can be committed to every day of the week. Consistency is crucial, even if you can manage only ten minutes a day in the beginning.

Strike a balance between structure and flexibility. There is no one way to have a quiet time. A little structure will help you avoid wasting time, while variety will keep you from getting bored.

Divide your time evenly between prayer and the Bible. You will have days when you have such a burning need to pray that it dominates, and others when God is speaking so strongly through Scripture that it dominates. But you should keep a rough balance.

Base your prayer on the Word, and saturate your Bible reading with prayer. For instance, before you read, ask God to enable you to understand what is written and hear what He wants to say to you. As you read, listen for what is revealed about God and what applies to you. When you are done, praise God for what you read about Him, thank Him for what He's done, ask Him for the grace to do what the passage commands, and invite Him to do what the passage describes in others' lives and your own. Use the passage as the basis for your petition, intercession, and praise.

Likewise, listen for God's voice during your prayer time, but remember that He won't ever contradict His written Word.

Write. Mark your Bible or take notes as you read. A simple approach is to choose one truth to focus on for the day, and to write it down or underline it. Then use this truth as the basis for your prayer time.

Many people find it helpful to list their prayer concerns or the names of the people they want to pray for. As prayers are answered, you can check them off on your list to remind yourself of God's eagerness to answer prayer. A list can be invaluable, but you should reorganize it or set it aside if it becomes a burden.

Be disciplined. Ask God daily for the strength to resist distractions, get enough rest, and keep your appointment with Him.

Follow a simple plan.[1] Consider using one of the following to help organize your quiet time. You can alternate for variety.

Plan A

- Be still for a moment before God (Psalm 46:10).
- Ask God to cleanse your heart and guide your time (Psalm 119:18; 139:23-24).
- Read a section of Scripture slowly, several times, at least once aloud. (This section should be the next one in your systematic plan of going through the Bible.) Meditate on the passage, and choose a verse to memorize.
- Write down what God has shown you.
- Take some time to praise God for who He is.
- Tell God about any sins you're struggling with, and ask for His power to abandon them. Ask what you should do.
- Pray for the needs on your list.
- Commit yourself and your day to the Lord.

Plan B

- Pray briefly about your quiet time, asking God to enlighten and guide you. Remind Him that your goal is to meet with Him and get to know Him better.
- Praise God, using 1 Chronicles 29:11-12 as a basis.
- Read part of a chapter or more, and choose a favorite verse.
- Use thoughts from your favorite verse as a starting point for each item on your prayer list.
- Dedicate your day to the Lord, and pray over its details.
- Conclude with a time of thanksgiving.

Plan C

- Read Psalm 143:8-10 as a prayer.
- Pray that you will thirst more for God and know Him more fully.
- Review verses you have memorized.
- Give thanks for special blessings, using a list of things for which you are thankful.
- Read the Word and prayerfully meditate, writing down a thought or two.
- Use the Lord's Prayer as a base from which to branch out in prayer for yourself and others.

WHAT IF MY QUIET TIME IS DRY?

Get enough rest.

Examine yourself. If God told you to do something three weeks ago and you haven't done it, or if you are practicing some sin without seeking to abandon it, then God won't tell you anything new until you act on what He has already said.

Don't rush.

Avoid ruts. Are you meeting a person or a habit? Is your quiet time an exercise to please a demanding God or to make yourself feel virtuous, or is it a chance to encounter the living Lord you love?

RESISTING TEMPTATION

No temptation has seized you except what is common to man. And God is faithful; he will not let you be tempted beyond what you can bear. But when you are tempted, he will also provide a way out so that you can stand up under it.

1 CORINTHIANS 10:13

DOES GOD TEMPT PEOPLE TO SIN?

The Bible uses the same words for testing and tempting. *God* tests His people to prove and strengthen their faith, trust, and loyalty. Trials strengthen spiritual muscles and form us into people fit for heaven. However, Satan's goal in tempting us in those trials is to damage trust and drive us to despair and to rebel. He uses the prideful desires inside us to coax us to sin. In reality, we tempt ourselves to sin when we toy with our corrupt desires, and Satan helps. God never tempts us to sin, but for our good He uses circumstances that He knows will try and test us (James 1:2-18; 1 Peter 1:6-7).

Our aim is to grow strong in trials rather than crumbling under them. Giving in even once weakens our ability to resist the next time (we take a step toward bondage), mars our intimacy with God, and encourages others to dishonor Him.

HOW CAN I RESIST TEMPTATION TO SIN?

Acknowledge that you are being tempted to sin and identify the sin.

Fix your eyes on Jesus. Meditate on how Jesus successfully dealt with temptations (Matthew 4:1-11; Luke 22:39–23:49; Hebrews 12:2-4).

Pray for God's strength to resist. Admit you lack the ability to resist the temptation, yet trust God to strengthen you if you humbly depend on Him (1 Corinthians 10:13).

Decide you are going to resist. Knowing that God will come through, commit your will to Him.

Flee or stand firm. Stay away from situations that you know are going to tempt you in your weak areas (2 Timothy 2:22). If you face one accidentally, run (Genesis 39:7-12). It's not showing courage to stay; it's demonstrating arrogant stupidity.

On the other hand, stand under persecution. To flee persecution is to capitulate to evil, to compromise the gospel.

Ally yourself with others fighting the same battle. One of the purposes of fellowship is to help each other resist sin. Meet regularly with a group of believers whom you trust, and talk and pray together about the temptations you each are facing. Support each other, and confess when you fall.

Meditate on the prize awaiting victors. Memorize and study Scriptures about your hope of eternal life and the glories of reigning with Christ (Romans 8:18-39; 1 Corinthians 15:50-58; Revelation 5:9-10).

Rejoice that the temptation is temporary and the victory is guaranteed. Don't flog yourself with guilt if you fail; just get up and keep fighting. God has everything under control, and He loves you and forgives you even when you fail.

DEPENDING ON GOD

*I am the vine; you are the branches. Those who remain in
me, and I in them, will produce much fruit. For apart from
me you can do nothing.*

JOHN 15:5, NLT

WHAT DOES IT MEAN TO DEPEND ON GOD IN DAILY LIFE?

Continue to work out your salvation with fear and trembling, for
it is God who works in you to will and to act according to his
good purpose. (Philippians 2:12-13)

To this end I labor, struggling with all his energy, which so
powerfully works in me. (Colossians 1:29)

We live the Christian life in one of these four ways:

1. *By our own effort and willpower.* We can do a lot of
    Christian activity and have apparent success, but we will
    often experience anxiety, burnout, and a lack of real fruit
    of the Spirit (Galatians 5:22-23). Our relationship with
    others will be hindered if we have pride in our own effort.

2. *"Let go and let God."* At the other extreme, we can do nothing at all. We won't feel stressed, but we also won't do any of the things God wants to accomplish through us.

3. *"Lord, help me."* Deep down where it counts, we feel that we can manage our Christian life up to a point, but after that we need God's help. We pray for God's help in the morning, then handle the day's ordinary tasks on our own. We call on the Lord if we hit a crisis. It is as though we found a log too heavy to lift and said, "Lord, if You will take one end, I will take the other and together we will lift this log."

4. *Constant active dependence.* We know that in reality we need God's enabling, not just His help, in every aspect of life. We pray for it constantly. Our prayer is, "Lord, You must enable me to lift this log if I am to do it. To all appearances it will seem as if I am lifting this log, and I truly am, but I am doing so only because You have given me all the strength to do it." The difference between (3) and (4) is partial versus total trust; we can easily slip from the latter to the former if we aren't careful. The difference between (2) and (4) is that in the latter we are using all our God-given faculties in a conscious effort to serve.[1]

Our heart attitude is what makes the difference in the fruit we bear, not saying the right words about total dependence.

KNOWING THE FAITH

Faith is that attitude in which, acknowledging our complete insufficiency for any of the high ends of life, we rely utterly on the sufficiency of God. . . . It is an act which is the negation of all activity, a moment of passivity out of which the strength for action comes, because in it God acts.

C. H. DODD, *THE MOFFATT NEW TESTAMENT COMMENTARY*

DISCOVERING GOD'S WORD

I am not ashamed of the gospel, because it is the power of God for the salvation of everyone who believes.

ROMANS 1:16

WHAT IS THE GOSPEL?

Gospel is an Old English word meaning "good news." The gospel is the good news God has announced concerning His Son (Romans 1:1-3). The news includes the following:

1. The Old Testament prophecies of the coming King have been fulfilled. Jesus has come into the world to rescue people "from the dominion of darkness" and to bring them into His kingdom (Colossians 1:13).

2. All people deserve God's wrath because we rebelled against His rule. Even when we tried to please Him, we failed because our hearts were corrupt and rebellious (Romans 1:18–3:20). Because of our rebellion, we were spiritually dead and under the control of Satan. But because of His great love for us, God the Father sent His Son, Jesus, to bear our guilt and sin on the cross to reconcile

us to Himself (Romans 3:21–5:21; Ephesians 2:1-7).

3.   Jesus was fully human, born in the royal line of David, and fully God as the Son of God (Romans 1:3-4), so He was able to be the perfect sacrifice and bridge between God and humanity. (See "Atonement," page 103.)

4.   Jesus was crucified, died, was buried, and was raised from death as prophesied (Matthew 27:27–28:15; 1 Corinthians 15:1-8). His resurrection is proof that He really is God's Son and that He really did overcome death for our sake.

5.   Jesus is now exalted with the Father and is Lord of all creation (Ephesians 1:20-23; Philippians 2:9-11).

6.   Jesus will return to earth to judge the world and bring to fulfillment His saving work (Matthew 16:27; 1 Thessalonians 4:13-18).

7.   Anyone who calls upon Jesus to be saved and who submits to Him as Lord will be freed from bondage to evil and fear, protected from condemnation, reborn and welcomed into God's family, and given all the blessings of eternal life and intimacy with the Father (Romans 8:1-2,15-17; 10:9-13; Ephesians 1:3-14; Hebrews 2:14-15).

WHAT IS IN THE BIBLE?

The word of God is living and active. Sharper than any double-edged sword, it penetrates even to dividing soul and spirit, joints and marrow; it judges the thoughts and attitudes of the heart. (Hebrews 4:12)

The Old Testament

A testament or covenant is an agreement between two parties that defines their relationship. The Old Testament is the record of God's dealings with Israel under the Old Covenant. The New Covenant supersedes the Old in many respects, but the Old remains the foundation of the New. You can't understand who God is and what Christ accomplished without understanding the Old Testament. We generally have divided the books of the Old Testament according to the traditional Jewish divisions.

THE LAW/TEACHING OF MOSES

Genesis–Deuteronomy (books that define God's covenant relationship with Israel as King and Father)

Genesis (the name means "beginning") tells us how the relationship between God and humanity got started. It introduces God as the Creator, a basic key to who He is. It also shows us the beginnings of man and woman, of sin and death, and of God's plan to redeem humans from the catastrophe caused by sin. Genesis traces the story of God's chosen family—the descendants of Abraham through Jacob—Israel—from their origins to their descent to Egypt. Every key theme of the Bible is rooted in Genesis.

Genesis is a *narrative* book; it consists mainly of factual stories that were told about real people. Their temptations, family traits, and actions exemplify what people are like, how God deals with them, and how we should or shouldn't act in similar circumstances.

Exodus ("departure") tells how God delivered Israel from slavery in Egypt and covenanted with the people to be their God if they would be His loyal subjects. This story reveals God's love and power, and it helps us understand how God delivered us from slavery to sin. Exodus contains the first installment of the laws the King gave His subjects so that they would be a just, compassionate, and ordered society. These laws contain valuable principles of love and justice for us. The instructions for building the tabernacle (God's royal tent for living in Israel's midst) teach us about how to worship a Holy God and hint at what Christ was going to do.

Leviticus instructs the priests (from the tribe of Levi) on how to perform each kind of sacrifice to God. The regulations graphically portray what Christ accomplished when He sacrificed Himself to bring us back into relationship with the Holy God. Other laws of cleanness and moral purity help us grasp what radical holiness implies.

Numbers shows Israel on the brink of inheriting all that God had to offer them but forfeiting that inheritance through faithlessness. An entire generation wanders and dies in the desert between Egypt and the Promised Land, yet God displays His faithful love by sustaining the people so that the next generation can receive the inheritance. Numbers is a portrait of God responding to human sin with His perfect balance of justice and love.

Deuteronomy is Moses' last words to Israel before his death. It is a moving call to faithfulness and a summary of the Old Covenant—how God's people were expected to treat Him and other people. Deuteronomy is one of the books Jesus quotes most often in the Gospels because He carries many of its principles over into the New Covenant.

THE FORMER PROPHETS

Joshua–2 Kings (books that evaluate Israel's history in light of the covenant)

Joshua tells how God fulfilled His promise to give Canaan to Israel. It is full of lessons for us about obedience, holiness, unity, courage, and God's ability to accomplish what He promises. Joshua illustrates concepts like inheritance and rest that recur in the New Testament.

Judges recounts how after Joshua's death, Israel lacked good leadership, so "every man did that which was right in his own eyes" (17:6, KJV). The result was a cycle of moral decay, political chaos, oppression by enemies, then cries for help and deliverance. We see that the Lord will not tolerate sin, even in His children, but that He is always waiting to deliver His children when they repent, humble themselves, and obey Him. We also see that chaos is inevitable when people are left to themselves.

Ruth is part of The Writings in the Jewish divisions, but Christian Bibles place it with Judges because it fits there in history. It is a beautiful story of love and loyalty in the midst of the faithless era of the judges. It shows how simple people can accomplish great things for God by living faithfully, how God cares about even our everyday griefs and joys, and how He chose a penniless foreign widow to become the ancestress of King David and Christ.

1 & 2 Samuel trace Israel's history from the low point at the end of Judges to the pinnacle of David's triumph to the tragedy of his later years because of his failures as a man and a father. We learn why God gave Israel a king and what kind of king God wanted to lead His people. David, the man who foreshadowed Christ as King, is highlighted in all his strengths and failings. He shows us how to be a man (or woman) after God's heart.

1 & 2 Kings evaluate each of David's successors and the nation as a whole on the basis of how faithful they were to the covenant with God. The split and collapse of Israel and Judah because of idolatry and immorality illustrate that the nation's welfare depended on faithfulness to the covenant, and that leaders are evaluated not by worldly success but by how well they represent God's purity and holiness to the world. Yet God protects the royal line of David not because of humanity's virtue but because He is faithful to His promise to send a descendant of David to be the Messiah.

THE WRITINGS

1 Chronicles–Song of Songs (books of stories, drama, and poetry that God gave Israel)

1 & 2 Chronicles recount the reigns of David, Solomon, and the kings of Judah until Judah's destruction. These books focus on the importance of worshipping God and living faithfully to His Word.

First and Second Chronicles portray Judah's good kings as fore-shadows of the Messiah.

Ezra and Nehemiah tell how God restored the exiled Jews to the Promised Land and enabled them to rebuild Jerusalem and the temple despite all obstacles. These books are a tribute to God's amazing faithfulness and the courage of a few committed believers.

Esther shows how God saved His people from yet another threat of destruction by placing a woman and her cousin in crucial positions. Their courage and faithfulness are more examples for us.

Job is a drama about the suffering of a man who loves and obeys God. It deals with questions such as: Why does God let suffering happen? Is God really as loving and just and powerful as the Bible says? Will people trust and serve God when there seems to be nothing in it for them?

Psalms contains 150 songs of praise and petition to God. The psalmists express to God their feelings from the depths of despair to the heights of exultation. Their words comfort, strengthen, enlighten, and lift us to worship in every circumstance.

Proverbs teaches us how to obtain wisdom, insight, and a morally disciplined life. The various proverbs address the nitty-gritty of business, relationships, entertainment, and even eating habits.

Ecclesiastes is a journal of one man's search for happiness, in all the wrong places, and his conclusions.

Song of Songs celebrates the beauty, power, and preciousness of human love in a committed marriage relationship. It also portrays the passionate love between God and His people.

The prophets describe graphically how God feels and what He does when we ignore Him. They also promise what He does (ultimately through Christ) when we turn to Him humbly.

THE LATTER PROPHETS

Isaiah–Malachi (books by prophets evaluating their present situations and foreseeing the future in light of the covenant)

Isaiah is the prophet most often quoted in the New Testament. Through him God unveils the scope of His plan to judge Israel for its sin, yet ultimately to save the world. Isaiah prophesies Jesus Christ's character and mission with precision.

Jeremiah calls Judah to repent in order to stay the coming judgment of destruction. He also reveals his intimate wrestlings with God. Jeremiah promises that although judgment must follow sin, a faithful remnant will be delivered by the Messiah under a new covenant.

Lamentations is a series of five poetic laments over the fall of Jerusalem. (The Jews consider it one of The Writings, but Christians include it with the Prophets.) The author, Jeremiah, weeps over his destroyed city. Yet he recognizes that God has treated Jerusalem as her wickedness deserved. Jeremiah also knows that because God is the Lord of hope, love, faithfulness, and salvation, He will respond when His people repent.

Ezekiel explains God's ways to a stiff-necked people, gives grieving exiles hope that God has not forgotten them, and presents a glimpse of the coming Messiah, the Holy Spirit, the forgiveness of sins, and the kingdom of God. Like Jeremiah, Ezekiel is a model of one who intercedes on behalf of his people.

Daniel is part of The Writings in the Jewish divisions, but it recounts the life and visions of a prophet. Daniel's career in a pagan government is a model for Christians in a secular world. His visions declare God's sovereignty and ultimate triumph over His enemies.

Hosea rebukes God's people for committing adultery against their Husband through the worship of wealth, sex, and power.

Joel foresees terrible judgment upon God's complacent people, yet restoration and abundance when the punished repent.

Amos, too, promises judgment for a materialistic, unjust nation.

Obadiah proclaims judgment for God's enemies.

Jonah is the unwilling evangelist. His life shows that the calling of God's people is to bring the unbelieving nations, whom God also loves, into His fold.

Micah speaks of more destruction and hope.

Nahum announces the destruction of the evil empire arrayed against God.

Habakkuk is a dialogue between the prophet and God. Habakkuk objects to the way God allows wickedness; God replies, and Habakkuk responds with renewed faith.

Zephaniah portrays the horrors of judgment and the hope of restoration.

Haggai promises that if the people put God first they will be blessed, but if they don't they will be cursed. Haggai gives a glimpse of the Messiah.

Zechariah motivates the people to rebuild God's temple and trust totally in Him. Zechariah foresees Christ's lowliness, humanity, rejection, crucifixion, priesthood, kingship, glory, and reign. God's sovereignty throughout history is emphasized.

Malachi speaks to people who doubt God's love because He seems inactive. He gives them reasons for faith and warns against losing hope.

The New Testament

THE GOSPELS

Matthew–Acts (books about Jesus' life and ministry)

Matthew reveals Jesus as the King promised by the Old Testament prophets and as the ultimate Teacher of God's truth.

Mark leads us to see who Jesus is by watching what He does, in serving people and in dying for them.

Luke emphasizes that Jesus came for the outcast, the poor, the non-Jews, and the sinners.

John stresses that Jesus is fully God and writes to draw unbelievers to faith.

Acts tells how the Holy Spirit spread the church across the Roman Empire after Jesus' departure. Acts portrays the church's mission, message, and methods; how Christians should react to opposition; and God's power to triumph over all obstacles.

PAUL'S LETTERS

Romans–Philemon (written to churches by the man who oversaw them)

Romans states the gospel systematically to show how it is "the power of God for . . . salvation" (Romans 1:16). Paul explains such key concepts as sin, grace, faith, how to become right with God, and how to grow in holiness.

1 Corinthians deals with such issues as spiritual pride, divisions between Christians, sexual morality, church discipline, marriage, ethical gray areas, public worship, spiritual gifts, the Lord's Supper, and the Resurrection.

2 Corinthians responds to teachers who were undermining Paul's authority. It addresses the nature of an apostolic ministry, authority, human weakness and Christ's strength, Paul's attitude toward painful circumstances, and his views on financial giving.

Galatians proclaims that active faith in Christ, not self-reliant effort to be good, is the way to become and to live as God's child.

Ephesians reveals God's eternal purpose and grace so that we may understand and live by God's glorious goals for His church. Our blessings in Christ, relationships with other believers, and spiritual warfare are all included.

Philippians is a message of joy in the midst of affliction. It presents a loving call to be humble, united with fellow believers, and firm against both legalism and licentiousness.

Colossians exalts Christ as fully God and upholds Christian freedom against legalism.

1 & 2 Thessalonians encourage new believers who are suffering trials, instruct them in godly living, and reassure them about what will happen when Christ returns.

1 Timothy counsels a young pastor (Timothy) on refuting false teachings, supervising his church, and appointing qualified church leaders.

2 Timothy exhorts Timothy to be bold in his ministry, despite opposition.

Titus counsels another young leader on dealing with opposition and false teaching, and on raising up a congregation that will make the gospel attractive to outsiders.

Philemon is a personal note that reflects Christian love and authority.

OTHER LETTERS

Hebrews–Revelation (written to believers by various apostles)

Hebrews encourages persecuted believers to hold on by explaining how Christ is utterly supreme as the bringer of God's grace. Along with Romans, it is the New Testament's best commentary on the Old Testament.

James tells us how to grow to mature, vital Christian living.

1 Peter gives hope amid persecution. It discusses such topics as who we are as Christians, holy living, and how to deal with authority.

2 Peter tells us how to deal with false teachers and evildoers within the church and how to grow in Christlikeness.

1 John explains how to be assured that we are God's children and how to discern false Christians from true ones.

2 & 3 John give two examples of how to live by both truth and love.

Jude warns against false teachers.

Revelation encourages believers to stand firm by assuring them that, although the forces of evil will have temporary victory, God will ultimately triumph and glorify those who are faithful even unto death.

GETTING THE MOST FROM THE BIBLE

All Scripture is God-breathed and is useful for teaching,
rebuking, correcting and training in righteousness.

2 TIMOTHY 3:16

WHY SHOULD I READ THE BIBLE?

God desires to talk with you. He can communicate to you through circumstances and as you pray, but the foundational and most reliable way He speaks is through the written words of the Bible. Those words are "God-breathed" — that's what *inspired* literally means. The Bible is an objective, trustworthy standard of God's will, character, and truth. The Bible is your best source if you want to know:

- Who God is
- What God desires
- What God offers
- God personally

The Bible tells you how to enter God's presence and live a secure, fruitful life in intimacy with Him.

HOW CAN I KNOW THAT THE BIBLE IS RELIABLE?

Human interpretations are fallible, but you can trust the facts and teachings in the Bible because:

Jesus said so (Matthew 5:18; John 10:34-35).

Prophecies reveal the Bible's supernatural origin. "The Bible made numerous predictions, sometimes hundreds of years in advance, that were literally and accurately fulfilled."[1]

Archaeology and historical documents confirm it. Critics have been unable to disprove a single detail, despite intense effort. The resurrection of Jesus—the fact on which the whole Book stands or falls—is amply attested, for any reasonable court of law.

The Bible has transformed more lives than any other book in the world.

It has "amazing unity amid great diversity."[2] The Bible was written by thirty-five authors (from peasants to kings) in two main languages over about 1,600 years. Yet it is one Book with one message, because God inspired every writer.

God confirmed its writers' authority. The authors were proven to be true prophets and apostles by the accuracy of their prophecies and the miraculous signs that accompanied their ministries.

The canonical councils were meticulous. The Hebrews and early Christians had innumerable books that were well regarded. But the canonical councils subjected every candidate for Scripture to rigorous tests as to author, facts, and doctrine. They prayed and pondered carefully, for they were not about to approve any books that were not unquestionably inspired by God.

WHAT SHOULD I REMEMBER ABOUT THE BIBLE WHEN I READ IT?

Take it seriously—it's divine. The Creator of the universe, the God who has rescued you from disaster, gave it. So, it deserves a humble, attentive, believing response. You can buy a Bible, but you don't own it in the sense of having the right to control what you will use from it. Its Author owns you. Let His words penetrate your defenses, show you the truth about yourself, transform what you think, and confront you with the Holy One.

Enjoy it—it's good news. Let it convict you, not depress you. Let it drive you into the arms of the One who has the power to make you into the person you want to be but can't. Let it draw you into the arms of the One who loves you.

Study it—it's personal. God didn't just dictate a series of sermons to secretaries. People in particular historical settings and with important purposes of their own wrote each book of the Bible. Therefore, to understand what God is saying through a book, we must determine what it meant when it was first written. This requires researching the historical and cultural background, and also reading and rereading the text.

HOW SHOULD I GO ABOUT READING THE BIBLE?

Read it daily. It's better to set aside fifteen minutes every day to let the Bible affect you than to try to manage an hour a day but fail most of the time. Start with an amount of time that you can live up to consistently, every day.

Read it systematically. If you read at random, you will tend to read only the parts you like and miss large portions that are unfamiliar or seem uninteresting. This will give you an unbalanced view of God. Instead, read straight through whole books. Alternate between the New and Old Testaments. If you have never read the entire Bible, start with a plan to read it all in a year (at the rate of two or three chapters a day), then go back and study individual books more closely. Various organizations publish plans for covering the Bible systematically if you need help. But you can make your own plan just by reading three chapters of Genesis a day until you finish it, then two chapters of Matthew every day, and so on.

Balance devotional reading and study. You might want to read for fifteen minutes a day, just to commune with God and hear His voice, then take an hour on Saturday or Sunday for careful study. Or you might want to read devotionally every day for a month, then take a couple of weeks to delve into a book with study aids. Alternating between a focus on study for careful interpretation and on prayerful listening to let God change you will keep your Bible reading fresh and balanced.

Don't treat the Bible as magic. God will sometimes guide you to the passage that speaks to the specific situation you are wrestling with. But beware of using the Bible like a Ouija board: opening at random and dipping your finger in, hoping to find the answer to a question. Beware of insisting that the passage you are reading today be the answer to today's concern. Instead, read systematically, and read today's passage for what God is saying through it. Write down and pray about what you learn. Let it sink in. If you want God's guidance on a specific issue, look back through your notebook or carefully search through your Bible for other passages that shed light on your question. Use a concordance or a topical Bible to research an issue, but avoid pulling individual verses out of context.

HOW DO I STUDY THE BIBLE?

Get an overview. Start by *reading a book at least once through*, preferably two to five times. Jot notes about your *first impressions*: What does the book seem to be about? Does the mood seem to be serious, humorous, joyful, mournful, rebuking, or encouraging? Does the author seem to be teaching doctrine, telling a story, exhorting his readers to do something, or writing for another purpose or purposes? How does the author seem to feel about his readers? What writing style is he using—poetry, a friendly letter, a sermon, episodes of a story? What words does he repeat often as clues to the ideas he is emphasizing?

Next, divide the book into *main sections*. These may not correspond to the chapter divisions. Give each section a title that summarizes its content.

Now you should have a good beginning grasp of the purposes for which the book was written. The author's original purpose often shows how God wants to use the book in your life. Try to *write a brief statement of what the book is about* and why you think it was written.

Once you have taken an overview, you are ready to observe various details in specific passages.

Observe. Observing details in a passage is a matter of asking and answering a lot of questions:

- *Who* is being addressed? Who is speaking? Who is being spoken of? (What do you know about these people?)
- *What* is the speaker saying? What is happening? What do you see?
- *When* is the action taking place? When is the predicted event going to occur?
- *Where* is the action taking place? Where will the event occur?
- *Why*, according to the author, is this statement true? Why is it important? Why did this happen?
- *How* is this promise possible?

Interpret. Once you've carefully observed what a passage says, consider what it means. Divide it into subsections and paragraphs. Think about what verses belong together and what subjects are covered. Then relate the paragraphs to each other. Ask yourself:

- What are the implications of the event?
- What do I think motivated this person to do this?
- What does this word mean?

One of the keys to interpretation is context. Interpret verses in light of the entire paragraph; interpret paragraphs in light of the entire book and the whole of Scripture. Take into account the type of literature the author has chosen, and interpret poetry under the rules of poetry, prophecy under the rules of prophecy, parables as parables, and letters as letters. (You may need to learn more about these types of literature.) Take into account the historical setting of the book as well. (Did a custom have some special meaning at the time? Was that statement made during a time of persecution or prosperity?)

Apply. The point of studying is to let God make you more like Christ. Gaining knowledge without acting on it will puff you up and make you like the Pharisees Jesus condemned (Matthew 23:27-28). So let the passage affect your life.

First, tell God you are ready to obey Him and ask Him how He wants this passage to affect your life. Then, ask yourself these questions.[3]

- Is there a *sin* here for me to confess or avoid? (Do I need to make restitution?)
- Is there a *promise* to claim and live by? (Does this promise apply to me, or just to the original readers? Have I met the conditions for claiming this promise?)
- Do I need to change an *attitude*? (How can I go about this?)
- Is there a *command* to obey? (Am I willing to do this no matter what I feel?)
- Is there an *example* to follow or avoid?
- Is there something to *pray* or *praise God* about?
- What *truth* can I learn about God the Father, Jesus Christ, or the Spirit? What difference should it make to me?

When you choose an application, listen to what God wants to do in your life, rather than to what you would like to achieve or concentrate on. This will require thought and prayer.

Summarize. When you've studied a book in detail, go back and see if your view of its main themes and purposes has changed. Write a short summary of what the book is about and how it is supposed to affect our lives.

Use resources. Ultimately, you must depend on the Holy Spirit to illuminate the Scriptures for you. But some basic resources are invaluable as you study to discern what the Spirit is saying:

An accurate translation of the Bible. Don't use a paraphrase as your primary version for study. It can be helpful as a commentary on the text, but you should go first to a literal translation. Take time to look at several versions in a bookstore before you choose one. You may find paragraph divisions and subtitles helpful.

A study Bible that includes cross-references and/or comments in the margins may be a good choice. Before you choose one, however, ask about its theological slant to be sure you won't be biased unknowingly toward someone's opinions.

A complete concordance. Young's and Strong's concordances list every word in the Bible alphabetically, along with each verse in which the word appears. A concordance can help you trace a theme (such as humility or prayer) through the whole Bible.

A Bible dictionary. Use this to look up historical and cultural background about a passage.

A one-volume commentary. This is a reasonably inexpensive source of what someone experienced thinks about a passage. Ask about the theological slant of commentaries before you buy one.

A Bible atlas. Geography had a huge impact on biblical events. You'll find places named in nearly every book of the Bible.

HOW DO I READ DEVOTIONALLY?

Pray. Before you start to read, ask God to speak to you personally through the passage. As you read, praise and thank God for things the passage says about His character or what He has done. Ask Him to make real in your life the things the passage says He wants to do. Make an effort to listen to God speaking.

Read the passage aloud. This helps the truths penetrate to your heart. If you are reading a story, get caught up in it. If it is a letter, let the author's feelings touch you.

Meditate on it. Meditation is "a piece of straight thinking under God's guidance and Godwards." It is digesting a scriptural truth by chewing on it over and over until you understand it and have drawn conclusions about how "to live more precisely and more concretely in accordance with the gospel."[4]

Here are some suggested steps for meditation:

- Ask yourself the observation and interpretation questions on page 88.
- Look closely at the scene, and speculate on what the people in the story might have been thinking and feeling.
- Read a sentence several times, emphasizing different words.[5]
  - "*I* can do all things through Christ . . ."
  - "I *can* do all things through Christ . . ."
  - "I can *do* all things through Christ . . ."
- Put the passage into your own words.
- Ask yourself the application questions on page 89.

Write out your thoughts about the meaning and your plan for application.

Memorize a key verse.

WHY DO I SOMETIMES FAIL WHEN I TRY TO APPLY A STATEMENT IN SCRIPTURE?

Peter said, "Rid yourselves of all malice and all deceit" (1 Peter 2:1). Perhaps you tried to do that for a few days and discovered that you are still deceitful and feel malice toward certain people. It helps to realize the following:

Change is a process. You built up the habit of deceit over years to protect yourself from hurt and achieve what you wanted. It is going to take God some time to uproot and replace such habits.

Let God control the process. Your old self was crucified with Christ when you accepted Him as your Lord, but your sinful nature fights to live on and stay in control. The sinful nature animates the habits such as malice and deceit that God wants to uproot. However, when you try hard to break those habits yourself, your sinful nature will sometimes cooperate. It will give up a certain amount of surface malice in order to maintain deep control of your life. But God is not so much interested in changing this or that bad habit as He is in taking complete control of your life, killing the old nature, laying a new foundation, and rebuilding you from the ground up. When you try hard to break a bad habit and fail, let the failure drive you to deeper dependence on God. Ask Him to make you more loving and honest, but more than that, thirst for Him to remake you in His image.

Let God reveal the root of your habits.

No good tree bears bad fruit, nor does a bad tree bear good fruit. Each tree is recognized by its own fruit. People do not pick figs from thornbushes, or grapes from briers. The good man brings good things out of the good stored up in his heart, and the evil man brings evil things out of the evil stored up in his heart. For out of the overflow of his heart his mouth speaks. (Luke 6:43-45)

If you have a bad fruit in your life, you can be sure that it is growing from a bad root in your heart. Your deceitful behavior may be rooted in a heart judgment that people will reject the real you, a heart anger against those who have rejected you in the past, or a heart commitment to get what you want regardless of how it affects others. As you study the Bible, pray, and talk with other believers, ask God to reveal those roots. When He convicts you, you will be able to see and reject your sin in all its ugliness.

Forgiving others is crucial. At the root of many of our destructive behaviors lies a refusal to forgive people who have hurt us. We have responded to hurt with bitterness and a resolve to protect ourselves from being hurt again. But when we refuse to forgive, we put up a wall that blocks God from forgiving and changing us (Matthew 6:14-15; 7:1-5). The only way to acquire traits such as love, joy, and peace is to forgive those who have wronged us and to stop protecting ourselves from hurt. This presumes that loving God is more important to us than holding on to bitterness, that loving others is more important than not hurting, and that we trust God to take care of us when we are hurt.

Knowing the Father is crucial. At the root of many destructive behaviors lies a desire to be nurtured. We all crave to be loved, valued, and respected, and none of us had perfect parents. We have sought nurturing from many wrong sources: sex, money, food, possessions, work, drugs, status, alcohol. The only way to become free of these false sources of nurture is to:

- Recognize them for what they are: rotten bread and polluted water
- Seek God as the Source of true bread (John 6:35-59) and living water (John 7:37-39)

The Spirit within us cries out, "*Abba*, Father." *Abba* means "Papa." We need to come to our Papa with the passion of deep hunger and thirst for the nurture only He can give.

If you need help, get it. Rarely can we let go of deeply rooted habits on our own. If you are struggling with a temptation or compulsion you can't shake, talk to a Christian or Christians you trust. The prayers and counsel of a friend may be enough to help you cling to the Father when you are tempted to go back to the habit. If you don't have a friend with the maturity to help you, or if your problem seems more than your friend can handle, seek professional Christian counsel.

WHAT DOES IT MEAN TO "CLAIM" BIBLICAL PROMISES, AND IS THIS VALID?

To "claim" a promise is to say (1) this promise applies to me, and (2) my actions are going to show that I trust God to keep this promise. It is valid to claim promises that truly apply to you. However, some promises in the Bible apply only to certain individuals or nations. God promised to make Abraham the ancestor of the Messiah; you can't claim that promise. To discern whether a promise applies to you, ask yourself:

- To whom does God make this promise in the original context of the passage? (To all people? All believers? Jesus' disciples? Israel? An individual?)
- Is there anything in the immediate context, the rest of the book, or elsewhere in the Bible that suggests that this promise applies to me?
- Are there any conditions attached to the promise? If so, have I met all of them?

If you aren't sure if a promise applies to you, ask someone with a mature knowledge of the Bible.

HOW CAN I TELL IF SOMEONE IS MISUSING THE BIBLE?

Ask yourself these questions:

Is some person's, group's, or book's interpretation of the Bible considered the real standard? In a cult, the leader(s) or some book other than the Bible (such as the *Book of Mormon*) is viewed as the real authority, and Scripture is interpreted in light of that other source. If you aren't permitted to challenge that other source, then the Bible is being misused even if the source's views on a particular subject happen to be biblical.

Does the interpretation contradict what the church has held to be true for two thousand years? Beware of groups who say that Scripture was misunderstood for all the many centuries until they came along.

Is the interpretation consistent with the whole of Scripture? You may not know the Bible well enough to answer this. If not, check with mature Christians *outside* the group in question.

DEVELOPING A CHRISTIAN WORLDVIEW

"I know the plans I have for you," declares the LORD, "plans to prosper you and not to harm you, plans to give you hope and a future."

JEREMIAH 29:11

Maybe you think you're not philosophical and aren't concerned with questions about "worldview." But your worldview lies at the root of all your values, priorities, and choices. It's up to you to develop your own answers to these questions as you grow in Christ. But here are some starting thoughts. If you read other sections of this book, you'll soon find that nearly every issue looks back to one or more of these basic worldview questions.

WHO AM I?
You are first of all a human being.

God said, "Let us make man in our image, in our likeness, and let them rule over the fish of the sea and the birds of the air, over the livestock, over all the earth, and over all the creatures that move along the ground." So God created man in his own image, in the image of God he created him; male and female he created them. . . . God saw all that he had made, and it was very good. (Genesis 1:26-27,31)

You are created in the image of God. Whether you are male or female, you bear the stamp of the Creator of the universe. You reflect His personality, His ability to make moral choices, His dignity and responsibility. You bear His authority over the rest of the earth and its inhabitants. You were created "very good." This means that you have value just for existing, and so does every other human being you encounter. This truth has far-reaching implications for the value of human life (Genesis 9:6), your ultimate loyalties (Luke 20:20-26), and even the words you utter (James 3:9-10).

> When I consider Your heavens, the work of Your fingers,
> The moon and the stars, which You have ordained;
> What is man that You take thought of him,
> And the son of man that You care for him?
> Yet You have made him a little lower than God,
> And You crown him with glory and majesty!
> You make him to rule over the works of Your hands;
> You have put all things under his feet. (Psalm 8:3-6, NASB)

You are "a little lower than God"—a creature, but a glorious one.

You are male or female. Your gender is not something incidental to you. At the very inception of Creation, God made humankind male and female. You express the image of God in your masculinity or femininity. You need to discover for yourself what it means to be fully man or fully woman.

You are fallen. You were born with the image of God marred in you (but not erased) (Genesis 6:5).

You are redeemed. If you have accepted the price Christ paid for humanity's rebellion and committed yourself to serving Him from now on, you are freed from the death penalty you earned (Ephesians 2:1-5).

You are God's son or daughter. You have not become just a slave in God's house. You have been restored to full sonship or daughterhood. You have the right to call the Lord of the universe "Abba" (Romans 8:15). You are coheir with Christ and your fellow Christians of everything your Father owns.

Right now, your Father is in the process of remaking you into the image that sin has marred (Romans 8:29). You still fall far short, but He loves you as if you were perfect. There is nothing you could do to make Him love you more. You are His.

The implications of this truth should shake you. You don't have to serve God out of fear that He will punish you as a bad slave if you fail; you can obey Him as a beloved Papa. Sin should be the last thing you want to do, because it grieves your Dad, mars the glorious image of God in you, and probably hurts someone else who bears the image of your Father. But when you do sin you can run to Papa's arms for forgiveness (Luke 15:11-32).

You are part of God's family. You are not just an isolated child of God. You have responsibilities to and for your brothers and sisters in God's family. On the other hand, you also have a lot to gain from getting involved in their lives.

WHY AM I HERE?

You exist to glorify God (Ephesians 1:12). You glorify God first of all simply by existing and reflecting His glorious image. As a human who was rebellious and fallen but is now redeemed and being restored to holiness, you also glorify God by demonstrating His mercy and love to the entire universe (Ephesians 3:10-11). The change in you since you became Christ's is an evidence of God's glory.

Further, you glorify God by doing the work He has planned for you (Ephesians 2:10). God is at war, reclaiming the fallen world for His kingdom. Each of His children has a crucial part to play in that war.

> As the Father has sent me, I am sending you. (John 20:21)

WHERE DID THE WORLD COME FROM?

God created it (Genesis 1:1). We can debate how long God took to create the world and the precise physics that took place, but the fact that God did it is basic. This fact means that nothing is an accident, and that nothing is inherently evil (Genesis 1:31).

God created it through Christ (John 1:3; Colossians 1:16). Christ is the Word of God, the agent of Creation, fully God.

WHAT'S OUT THERE BEYOND THE WORLD?

First and foremost, God is out there. He is a person, not a "force." He is one God in three Persons: Father, Son, and Holy Spirit.

Second, out there are all sorts of beings that are not part of the physical universe. The Bible calls them angels, "thrones or powers or rulers or authorities" (Colossians 1:16), and "the spiritual forces of evil in the heavenly realms" (Ephesians 6:12). Some are God's servants, while others are in rebellion against Him. At the head of the rebels is a fallen angel called Satan — the Adversary, the Accuser. God created him, so he is in no way God's equal.

God and His angels, along with Satan and his supporters, are involved in what goes on in the world of humans. In fact, these two groups are engaged in an all-out war for control of the universe. Satan is called "the prince of this world" (John 12:31), because he rules fallen humans and the world systems they live under. But the Father sent Christ to rescue people from "the dominion of darkness" and bring them into His own kingdom (Colossians 1:13).

The moral and spiritual struggle that goes on within each human and between humans is part of the cosmic struggle between God's kingdom and Satan's. Both sides are at work influencing men and women to join their camp. God permits His followers to use only measures that guard the individual's dignity, while Satan and his cohorts use unscrupulous tactics. The implications of this battle for your life are far-reaching:

> Our struggle is not against flesh and blood, but against . . . the powers of this dark world and against the spiritual forces of evil in the heavenly realms. (Ephesians 6:12)

Even when it looks like certain people are your enemies, your real foes are Satan and his demons. The demons' tools of bondage are fear, unforgiveness, compulsive habits, wrong beliefs, and oppressive social and political structures.

The weapons we fight with are not the weapons of the world. On the contrary, they have divine power to demolish strongholds. We demolish arguments and every pretension that sets itself up against the knowledge of God, and we take captive every thought to make it obedient to Christ. (2 Corinthians 10:4-5)

Our weapons for demolishing "strongholds" (the tools of bondage) are prayer, God's Word, and the power and love of God who lives inside us. The armor that protects us against attack in this battle is God's truth, Jesus' righteousness, the gospel, faith in Christ, and assurance of salvation, as well as prayer and Scripture (Ephesians 6:13-18).

DEFINING IMPORTANT CHRISTIAN TERMS

Do not let this Book of the Law depart from your mouth;
meditate on it day and night, so that you may be careful to
do everything written in it. Then you will be prosperous and
successful.

JOSHUA 1:8

Atonement. God's provision for restoring sinful humans to a blessed relationship with Himself. Sin separates a person from God and makes him or her deserve death. In the Old Testament, God provided a complex system of sacrifices to atone for (cover, satisfy the price of) sin. Animals were killed to take the place of the people who deserved the death penalty. That substitution was valid because God declared it to be a just exchange. However, the animal sacrifices pointed forward to the true substitutionary death—Jesus' death on the cross.

We can look at atonement in several ways: (1) Christ ransoms (redeems) us from slavery to sin and death. (2) Christ breaks our connection with Adam, from whom we get our sinful nature (we still have the sinful nature, but its power has begun to be broken). (3) Christ paid the penalty for our sin, so we are declared "not guilty" in God's court of justice. (4) Christ appeased God's holy wrath against sin by taking that wrath upon Himself unto death. (5) Our sinful nature was crucified with Christ. (6) Christ overcame the evil world order by dying and rising from the dead. (7) Christ reconciles us to the Father by doing away with the hostility that sin aroused in us.[1]

Baptism. The rite that declares publicly that a new birth into union with Christ has taken place (Romans 6:1-5; Galatians 3:7). Just as burial is a public declaration that someone has died, so baptism declares that someone has died spiritually with Christ and been raised to new life in Him. It signifies union with Christ and with His body, the church; entry into the kingdom of God; and a commitment to live under God's rule.

Church. The people of God gathered to worship and serve Him. It is Christ's very body. As Christians are united with Christ individually, they are also united with each other. They can't worship or serve Christ independently of each other. It is the community of the Spirit, who teaches, leads, gifts, and binds it together.

Conversion. Literally, to turn back. That is, to turn away from sin and self, and to turn toward God through Jesus Christ. At some point in the process of turning, God gives the believer new birth and eternal life. Rebirth completes conversion in one sense but in another sense conversion is a lifelong process.

Covenant. A political treaty, friendship pact, marriage contract, legal testament, or other agreement of relationship. God covenanted with Israel: "I will take you as my own people, and I will be your God" (Exodus 6:7). He thus became Israel's Sovereign, Friend, and Husband. The people did nothing to earn this gesture, but they received the blessings of the covenant only when they obeyed God. When Israel broke her allegiance to God, He punished her, but then established the New Covenant. The New is better than the Old because (1) it is sealed by a greater sacrifice, Jesus' blood; (2) it is open to all people, not just Jews; and (3) it offers us the power of the Holy Spirit to keep our side of the agreement.

Death. In the Bible, *physical death* is the permanent stopping of bodily functions. *Spiritual death* is "man's natural alienation from God, his lack of responsiveness to God, or his hostility to God, because of sin." *The second death* "refers to the permanent separation from God that is the destiny" of those who never turn back to God. Death to sin is suspending "all relations with sin" by "being alive to God through dying and rising with Christ" (see Romans 6:4-11). "Physical and spiritual death is the consequence and penalty of sin." For a Christian, physical death is (1) an evil brought by sin, (2) a tragedy in which the body is destroyed, (3) a good in which we rest from labor and entrust ourselves to God, and (4) a glorious hope in which we go to be with the Lord in sweet intimacy. Believers expect to be resurrected with undecaying spiritual bodies infused with the life of God. Thus, we should neither seek nor fear death. For an unbeliever death means facing his enemy, God, so we should pray for him to repent before he loses the chance.[2]

Dying with Christ means giving up all effort "to find life independently by our own efforts." We die to the world as a source of independent life and embrace the Father as the source of life. The Christian's freedom from death means liberty from "a death-bringing obligation continually to justify oneself." We can give freely to other people because we are secure that God accepts us and is sustaining us. Physical death remains for Christians to keep us depending on God for current and ultimate survival (see Faith).[3]

Faith. (1) Belief in a set of truths or (2) trust in a person because of a personal relationship. Both are crucial: "Without faith it is impossible to please God" (Hebrews 11:6). Faith is not a work that earns salvation; rather, we are saved "by God's grace operating through faith."[4] Faith is both a gift from God and an attitude we choose to adopt. It is not a "blind faith" that flies in the face of evidence. It is a decision (enabled by God and chosen by us) to hold on to the truth and relationship based on evidence, even when feelings and circumstances tempt us to give up. It is not closing the mind to reality, but opening it to the reality we have been doing our best to deny. Real faith in Christ inevitably leads to actions that conform to His character and commands, so faith that doesn't affect a person's behavior is "dead" (James 2:26).

Doubt may or may not equal unbelief. A believer may ask piercing questions in order to know more fully, or may struggle with why God is doing or allowing something. A questioner who wants to trust and understand God in humility should be supported. Someone with weak faith should be encouraged with love and biblical truth to trust God amid discouraging circumstances. However, sinful doubt comes from (1) pride in one's intellect or (2) unwillingness to accept the change in life and heart that accepting Christ's lordship would require. Unbelief is a matter of the will, not the mind. Honest doubt involves emotions, intellect, morals, and experiences. One should take care to find the root of someone's doubt before dealing with it.

The Fall. The first man and woman were created with the capacities to grow into God's moral character, to reason flawlessly, to choose freely, and to become immortal. When they chose to try to sustain their own lives apart from God, they and their descendants "fell" from the state of blessedness. Their moral natures became flawed, and they couldn't acquire godly character if they tried. Their minds became unable to perceive God and spiritual things accurately. Their freedom of choice became bound by unruly emotions, compulsions, and satanic control. They died spiritually, then later physically. Only through Christ's atonement is the Fall overcome.

Freedom. Christ came to liberate people from spiritual bondage to sin, the Law, fear, and death. Even when one is allowed to indulge every whim, he or she can still be enslaved to sinful compulsions and inevitable death. One can be a slave or under a totalitarian regime and yet be free in Christ from having to sin or die permanently. The only way to escape sin, the slave driver, is to die with Christ and be raised with Him to live as God's willing slave.

The Law acts as a babysitter, imposing rules without giving the power to obey. When we submit to Christ, our Father declares us adults who are free to serve Him without the babysitter hanging over us. We have the power and desire to obey inside us. The church doesn't (or shouldn't) force us to follow rules; we voluntarily restrict our freedom when love requires us to do so. Serving God is real freedom from the compulsion to feed and protect self. At the final resurrection, we and the whole earth will reach the fulfillment of our freedom from decay (Romans 8:21).

Grace. The undeserved favor of God to man because He loves and chooses us. He saves and enables us to become like Him by grace (as a gift of love).

Cheap grace is the idea that we can sin and reap no consequences because God will forgive us when we confess. The Bible responds: (1) God's grace isn't cheap; it cost Jesus dearly. No one who loves Christ willingly casually inflicts suffering on Him. (2) God is holy; He hates sin. If we love Him, we won't do what He hates. (3) We fled to Christ and died with Him in order to escape the bondage of sin. Who in his right mind would choose to go back to that slavery once he had been freed? (4) Confession is empty if it is not an expression of repentance. (5) "God cannot be mocked. A man reaps what he sows" (Galatians 6:7). We may escape eternal death by throwing ourselves on God's mercy, but God usually lets us reap partial (even severe) consequences of our actions to teach us maturity.

Guilt. The state of having committed a crime. It is not the same as feeling guilty; you can be guilty without feeling guilty, and vice versa. Guilt is not removed by removing the feeling of guilt, nor by canceling the penalty. God's forgiveness because of Christ's atonement means that we are freed not just from the penalty and not just from the feeling, but also from the guilt. A child of God is a cleansed criminal, reborn without guilt. When we sin as Christians, we are cleansed of guilt as soon as we confess.

Immortality. Only God has within Himself inexhaustible life. Humans were created with the potential to become either mortal or immortal, depending on how they responded to God. They became mortal through sin.

At the end of this age, all people will be resurrected. Those who turned to Christ while on earth will receive immortality of soul and body. Those who did not will receive "eternal death" (the meaning is debated, but it isn't good). "Souls" are not inherently immortal; they become immortal when the person (body, soul, and spirit) is resurrected.[5]

Christianity rejects reincarnation—people live and die on earth once, then are resurrected and judged (Hebrews 9:27). For the believer, "life after death" means going immediately to be with the Lord and eventually (or immediately) receiving one's glorified body. For unbelievers "life after death" is "a state of anguish and torment . . . as they await resurrection—and final judgment."[6]

Judgment. When Christ returns to earth, all people will be judged: living and dead, Christian and non-Christian (Acts 10:42; Romans 14:10-12). Judgment will be according to what we have done (Matthew 16:27; Romans 2:6; 1 Corinthians 3:10-15). Our works will be the evidence of whether God's free gift of salvation has been at work in our lives. (There is no way to counterfeit the evidence of rebirth by grace.) God's judgment of whether we belong to Christ will be fair because we will have chosen whether to respond to Christ and accept His grace (John 3:19-20). Those who have chosen Christ will be rewarded by eternally living with Him; those who have rejected Him will be eternally excluded from His presence. In love, God has provided everything we need to appear before Him guiltless and be blessed; it is up to us to accept His loving gift.

Kingdom of God. The present and future reign of God in Christ. God is the rightful King over the entire universe. However, first some angels and then all humankind rebelled. Because God had put humankind in charge of the world and humankind turned it over to Satan, the world and humankind came under the domain of Satan. God's strategy of regaining His territory by love rather than force is designed to cause all the universe to glorify Him as the King truly deserving of glory and praise. God began by choosing one nation, Israel, to be His "kingdom of priests" (Exodus 19:6), the foothold from which He would reconquer humankind. Through the Law and prophets, He outlined the kingdom society He desired. Then He sent Jesus, a descendant of Israel's human king and also the Son of the Great King Himself. Jesus proclaimed that the kingdom (reign) of God had arrived because He, the King, had arrived in the flesh. The blessings of the kingdom (healing, freedom, Satan's defeat, abundant life, relationship with the King) are available *now*. Yet they are available only as a foretaste, the first installment of what will come when Christ returns. His first coming was *incognito*. We now battle as in occupied territory. But our ultimate victory is assured: He will come again undisguised to reign, and we will reign under Him.

Law. God's commands recorded in the Bible. To break one of those commands is to prove that you are a sinner, for a sinner is incapable of obeying perfectly. The gospel declares that Jesus kept the Law in our place and died for our failure to keep it, and that we can be reconciled to God by putting faith in Jesus.

The purpose of the law is to: (1) guide society in promoting a just civil order, (2) convict people of sin and so drive them to Christ, and (3) teach Christians how to live in ways that honor God. Because Christ fulfilled the ceremonial law of the Old Covenant, Christians do not perform it. However, the New Covenant reaffirms or assumes the legal principles and moral commands of the Old. These continue to be wise guides for society and crucial standards for holy living.

Predestination. The idea that God has already decided who will and won't receive eternal life. Romans 8–11 and Ephesians 1 definitely teach this, but interpretations vary: (1) God knows who will respond to the gospel and has predestined to salvation those whom He knows will respond with faith and obedience; (2) humanity's fallen will is so corrupted that on his or her own a person can't choose to respond to the gospel in faith. In grace, God seeks and saves some sinners and not others. He chooses some, not because they are better in some way than the others, but simply because He chooses. It is not unjust for God to leave some sinners in the sin they chose; the miracle is that He saves anyone.

It is essential to hold both sides of the paradox—God's choice and humankind's responsibility—in tension. God commands evangelism to unbelievers and nurture of fellow Christians, and He holds us accountable for our responses. Yet nothing we do can thwart His will.

Regeneration. Rebirth into God's family, which takes place when a person puts his or her faith in Christ. It happens by God's Spirit, not human effort. It happens once-for-all in someone's life. In rebirth, God becomes your Father, you become His child, you gain the capacity to grow up to be like Him (holy and Christlike), and you become coheir to all He owns (along with Christ and your other siblings). Other Christians are your brothers and sisters, and you are expected to treat them with the sacrificial commitment of a real family.

Repentance. The biblical word signifies "to change one's mind," "to change one's feelings," and "to turn around." Thus, repentance involves grief about one's sin, a new thinking about what one is doing, and a decision to go God's way. Repentance involves emotions, intellect, and above all, will. It means saying to God, "You are right" about what You deserve, what I deserve, and what I should do now. Feeling remorse without a change in behavior isn't repentance. Even Judas felt remorse (Matthew 27:3-5). Likewise, conforming behavior without transforming attitudes and motives is not repentance, but legalism.

The inner conviction, new thinking, and power to change direction are all gifts of God. Repentance should be a daily habit as we constantly turn away from old ways toward God's ways.

Righteousness. *Righteousness* and *justification* reflect the same Greek and Hebrew words. They refer to "behavior in conformity with the covenant requirements,"[7] right standing in a covenant community, or the status of being declared in the right by a court of law.

God is righteous by nature; He always acts by the standards He laid down for Himself in His covenants. Because He promised to deliver and protect those who seek Him, He does it. Because He promised to judge sin, He did it by the Cross and will do it when Christ returns. Jesus' work is a demonstration that God is righteous both in dealing with sin and saving the helpless.

Humans are not righteous by nature. We have continually broken our covenant with God. However, by grace God imputes Jesus' righteousness to those who put their faith in Him. To attain right standing in the community of God, we need simply to believe the gospel. To be acquitted in God's court, we need only plead that we belong to Jesus. Real believers, of course, will go on to grow in righteous behavior by God's power. They will seek to treat others righteously—with justice—because they want to act like people who belong to Jesus.

Salvation. God's gracious act of delivering people from the wrath they deserve, from bondage to sin, Satan, and death. Also, the condition of total well-being that results from having been delivered. It is a shorthand word for all the blessings God bestows on believers. We "have been saved" when we converted (Ephesians 2:5,8); we "are being saved" (1 Corinthians 1:18); and we will be saved when Christ brings the kingdom in its fullness (Romans 13:11).

Sanctification. The act of setting something apart as holy; "the act or process by which people or things are cleansed and dedicated to God, ritually and morally."[8] Under the Old Covenant, priests, temple utensils, and animals were cleansed ritually and dedicated to God for exclusive use or sacrifice. This symbolized the inner, moral cleansing and dedication that God also wanted. The New Testament emphasizes this moral dimension.

On the one hand, to become a Christian is to allow God to permanently set you apart for Himself, to cleanse you from sin's defilement, and to dedicate you for His service. In that sense, we are already "saints" (holy ones, sanctified ones). On the other hand, we have submitted to a lifelong process of being made increasingly clean from sin and ever more yielded to God's service. Again, on one hand, only God can make us holy. Yet, on the other hand, God exhorts us to offer ourselves to Him as willing servants and living sacrifices (Romans 6:13,19; 12:1), to pursue holiness (Hebrews 12:14), and to act like holy people. Thus, holiness is both our *present* state and *future* goal, something we *passively* let God do in us and something we must *actively* pursue. We pursue it by constantly saying yes to God's commands and control of our lives and no to our selfish desires, by choosing to do the good He asks of us in total dependence on Him rather than on self.

Sin. The condition that separates humans from the Holy God. It is rebellion against God's desires, caused by the desire to be independently wise and powerful (Genesis 3:4-6), which is caused by pride. It is rejection of God's humility in Christ, His will that humankind be exalted yet submitted to Christ, and His offer of faithful love. The root of pride is linked to refusal or incapacity to believe that God is really so good, wise, and holy that He deserves utter allegiance.

Humankind is a unity, a family, a single organism. Adam, the legal head of humanity, declared independence from God, and all of his descendants are born into a family at war, and we soon confirm our heritage by committing acts of rebellion. The only way to escape the penalty for traitors is to surrender to the lawful King. This entails renouncing Adam's family heritage and joining ourselves securely to Christ as limbs of His body and offspring of His family. The Bible describes this as being "united with Christ" or "in Christ" rather than in Adam.

HAVING ASSURANCE IN CHRIST

I am convinced that neither death nor life, neither angels nor demons, neither the present nor the future, nor any powers, neither height nor depth, nor anything else in all creation, will be able to separate us from the love of God that is in Christ Jesus our Lord.

ROMANS 8:38-39

HOW CAN I BE SURE THAT I'M SAVED?

In his first letter, the apostle John gives some tests so that we can know we are reborn as God's children.

Belief.

Who is the liar? It is the man who denies that Jesus is the Christ. . . . Every spirit that acknowledges that Jesus Christ has come in the flesh is from God. (1 John 2:22; 4:2)

John is saying that a Christian believes that:

- Jesus is the anointed King promised by God.
- Jesus is the divine Son of God.

- Jesus is fully human.
- As both God and man, Jesus died on the cross for our sins. (See the summary of the gospel on pages 69–70.)

Walking in light.

God is light; in him there is no darkness at all. If we claim to have fellowship with him yet walk in the darkness, we lie. . . . But if we walk in the light . . . we have fellowship with one another, and the blood of Jesus, his Son, purifies us from all sin. If we claim to be without sin, we deceive ourselves. . . . If we confess our sins, he is faithful and just and will forgive us our sins and purify us from all unrighteousness. (1 John 1:5-9)

Everyone who has this hope in him purifies himself, just as he [Jesus] is pure. (1 John 3:3)

Children of God have been reborn with their Father's spiritual genes ("seed" in 1 John 3:9). They want to grow up to be just like their Dad, and they have the capacity to do it.

Walking in the light means:

- Desiring earnestly to be rid of all sin
- Resisting sin
- Confessing sin when we are aware of it
- Trusting God to forgive and cleanse us when we confess

Obedience.

We know that we have come to know him if we obey his commands. (1 John 2:3)

God's children want to obey Him, because they know and love Him well enough to understand that His commands are wise and good.

Love.

Whoever does not love does not know God, because God is love. (1 John 4:8)

If anyone has material possessions and sees his brother in need but has no pity on him, how can the love of God be in him? Dear children, let us not love with words or tongue but with actions and in truth. (1 John 3:17-18)

These verses are not meant to condemn you even though you are not yet perfect in obedience and love. They are meant to reassure you when your heart (or the Devil) condemns you (see 1 John 3:19-20). A newborn Christian is a spiritual baby just beginning to show love and obedience, to walk in the light, and to believe in Christ. The mark of a Christian is that he or she fervently *desires* to grow in these areas and is showing signs, however new, of such growth.

CAN I TELL IF SOMEONE ELSE IS SAVED?

Only God knows for certain, and we are not to condemn each other. However, we are supposed to evaluate the genuineness of others, especially of those who want to teach or lead.

> Watch out for false prophets. . . . By their fruit you will recognize them. (Matthew 7:15-16)

The fruits or signs of a prophet (or teacher) whom you can trust are right doctrine about Christ, walking in the light, obedience to God's commands revealed in Scripture, and active love for other Christians.

CALLED TO BE SENT

The evangelistic harvest is always urgent. The destiny of men and of nations is always being decided. Every generation is strategic. We are not responsible for the past generation, and we cannot bear the full responsibility for the next one; but we do have our generation. God will hold us responsible as to how well we fulfill our responsibilities to this age and take advantage of our opportunities.

BILLY GRAHAM

SHARING YOUR FAITH

You are the light of the world. A city on a hill cannot be
hidden. . . . Let your light shine before men, that they may
see your good deeds and praise your Father in heaven.

MATTHEW 5:14,16

WHAT IS EVANGELISM?

The Greek word *euangelion* means "good news" or "gospel." To evangelize, then, is to spread the good news about Jesus Christ. A related term Christians use is "witness." Witnesses are people who testify to what they know about a person or incident. Christians are witnesses to who Jesus is and what He does in people's lives. Evangelism includes making disciples of Jesus who obey Him and bringing people to repentance (Matthew 28:18-20; John 20:21-23; Acts 2:38-42).

Evangelism is supernatural.

The Spirit of the Lord is on me,
    because he has anointed me
    to preach good news to the poor.
He has sent me to proclaim freedom for the prisoners
    and recovery of sight for the blind,

to release the oppressed,

to proclaim the year of the Lord's favor. (Luke 4:18-19)

The Bible describes the non-Christian as spiritually blinded (Colossians 1:13; 2 Corinthians 4:4). Unbelievers cannot give sight to their own spiritual eyes, nor can a Christian through the Christian's own abilities. Your skill in explaining or arguing for the gospel is not what it takes to give sight to the spiritually blind. Consider Paul's approach to evangelism: "not with wise and persuasive words, but with a demonstration of the Spirit's power, so that your faith might not rest on men's wisdom, but on God's power" (1 Corinthians 2:4-5).

You have Christ's authority and His Spirit's anointing to be a supernatural resource for spreading the gospel.

Evangelism is a process of showing and telling.

You are the light of the world. A city on a hill cannot be hidden. Neither do people light a lamp and put it under a bowl. Instead they put it on its stand, and it gives light to everyone in the house. In the same way, let your light shine before men, that they may see your good deeds and praise your Father in heaven. (Matthew 5:14-16)

Both *witness* and *evangelize* suggest verbal declaration. But there is much more to spreading the gospel than just telling people what we believe. We must also *show* them through our lives that Jesus is who the Bible says He is.

We can compare the process of witnessing to that of farming.

In Mark 4:1-20, Jesus compares potential believers to soil. If we want the gospel to bear fruit in a person's life, we must first *cultivate* the soil by speaking to a person's heart through relationship, through caring for him or her. We can then *sow* the seed of God's Word, speaking verbally to the mind. Finally, we *reap* the harvest of a redirected life by asking the person to respond with his or her will. A real, healthy conversion requires that a person be emotionally attracted, intellectually convinced, and willing to submit control of his or her life to Christ.

The process involves mini-decisions. Think of a line starting at the foot of the Cross and stretching into the distance. The non-Christians you know are all somewhere on this line, at different distances from embracing the Cross and committing their lives to Christ. Some understand the gospel and just need to make a decision of their will. Others are attracted to your character and are wondering why you are different. Others are indifferent to you and your beliefs.

In attracting non-Christians to Christ, we should not focus on getting them to understand and decide about the gospel as quickly as possible. Instead, our goal is to help them make mini-decisions that gradually lead toward the Cross. In order to help a person make the next step toward Christ, it is crucial to know where he or she is on the line. Here are some of the mini-decisions we would like to lead a friend through:

- "He's okay" (a decision about us).
- "I'd like to get to know him better."
- "I'm going to find out why he's so different."

- "It seems that he gets his outlook on things from the Bible."
- "He's a Christian, but he's okay."
- "Being a Christian sure has its advantages."
- "I like his friends. I envy their confidence."
- "It might be interesting to look at the Bible someday."
- "The Bible isn't impossible to understand after all."
- "The Bible says some important things."
- "What the Bible says about life fits my experience."
- "Jesus seems to be the key. I wonder who He really was."
- "Jesus is God."
- "I need to do what He says."

Demonstration. Notice that the first three decisions are mainly about you as a person. As you demonstrate the gospel by showing love and grace to non-Christians, their hearts begin to be drawn toward you, so they become receptive to your outlook on life. The first aspect of demonstration is simply *showing love*. You make friends with people and treat them with respect and affection, regardless of the sins they practice.

At this stage, two of God's supernatural resources are in play. As you invite *God's Spirit* into the situation through persistent prayer, He goes to work in your friend's life. As you let God love your friend through you, *you* are God's representative.

The second aspect of demonstrating the gospel is *shining faith and hope* into your friend's life. You do this by having casual conversations on topics that reveal your values and his (topics such as success, work, leisure, marriage, children, or money). In such a conversation, you should:

- Ask and listen receptively to what your friend thinks about a given issue
- Give your own biblical opinion in a nonjudgmental way

When you have been friends for a while, you can mention that you get your views from the Bible.

Conversations on relevant topics will arise naturally as you do things with your friend—have lunch, jog, work on a project together. In your initial conversations, look for common ground on which to build a friendship. At the same time, you may want to introduce your friend to other Christians in ordinary social settings. Show your friend that you aren't the only loving, interesting Christian in the world.

In order to converse on important life issues, you need to have a biblical perspective on them yourself. The last section of this book may help you launch a personal study on a topic that is relevant to non-Christians.

Proclamation. Having identified yourself as a person who both loves and thinks, and who gets his or her ideas from the Bible, suggest that you can get together someday to look at the Bible. Your friend may find the idea threatening, so just toss it out there without trying to set a date. Once you've done this two or three times, over the course of a month or so, your friend will start getting used to it. After your friend shows genuine interest, set a date.

Now God's third supernatural resource is brought into play: *the Bible*. It's still not time to present the gospel and ask your friend to make a decision about Christ's offer of salvation. Instead, get together in a comfortable setting and look at a book of the

Bible together. Jim Petersen's book *Living Proof: Sharing the Gospel Naturally* (NavPress, 1988) gives thorough suggestions for how to lead a non-Christian through a study of the Bible in a nonthreatening way. It may take weeks or months, but eventually — supernaturally — your friend will come to see who Jesus is and what response He asks of people. Chances are you won't even be present when your friend finally makes a decision for or against Jesus.

THE BODY OF CHRIST

The holiest moment of the church service is the moment when God's people—strengthened by preaching and sacrament—go out of the church door into the world to be the church. We don't go to church; we are the church.

Canon Ernest Southcott

HAVING FELLOWSHIP WITH OTHER BELIEVERS

Make every effort to keep the unity of the Spirit through the bond of peace. There is one body and one Spirit—just as you were called to one hope when you were called.

EPHESIANS 4:3-4

WHAT IS FELLOWSHIP?

Fellowship (also translated "communion," "communication," "contribution," and "participation") comes from a Greek root meaning either "to have a share in" or "to give a share in." It means to be an *active* part of something—a business, a friendship, a marriage, or an encounter with a god. Having fellowship with Christ doesn't just mean being part of His family. It means that He is actively involved with us, that we are actively sharing in the day-to-day affairs of His business (establishing the kingdom of God), and that we are actively sharing in the lives of our colleagues (other Christians). Fellowship with other believers means:

Relationship—belonging to each other, sharing the life of God that we have because His Spirit lives in us.

Communicating on a close personal and spiritual level—sharing what God is teaching us through the Bible, sharing our struggles and the insights they are giving us about God, and encouraging each other to live as Christ would in our struggles. The focus and glue of our relating and communicating is God, His Word, and His works in our lives.

Partnership—We are partners in the business of the kingdom (Philippians 1:5).

Sharing material possessions (Acts 2:44-45)—Limbs of a single body, blood relatives, and business partners take care of each other.

HOW IS FELLOWSHIP WITH OTHER CHRISTIANS RELATED TO FELLOWSHIP WITH GOD?

To be a Christian is to be:

- A branch of the vine, Christ (John 15:1-8)
- A limb of His body (1 Corinthians 12:1-26)
- A reborn child of the Father (John 1:12-13)

We are united with Him so intimately that our identity and even our life depend on Him. We have fellowship with each other because we are branches of the same vine, limbs of the same body, and children of the same Father. Those who love their Father naturally love His other children.

If one part suffers, every part suffers with it; if one part is honored, every part rejoices with it. (1 Corinthians 12:26)

WHY DO I NEED A CHRISTIAN COMMUNITY?

Christians in the United States live in an individualistic culture. It's tempting to think we can make it with Christ alone. But you need other Christians . . .

To help you grow more like Christ. Look at the traits in which the New Testament says we should grow: love, faithfulness, forgiveness, peace, kindness, gentleness, self-control, patience, joy. Nearly all of these traits deal with relationships. Believers to whom you have deeply opened your life will drive you to levels of forgiveness of which you never dreamed.

To help you testify to the truth of the gospel. Jesus said, "By this all men will know that you are my disciples, if you love one another" (John 13:35). For all believers He prayed, "May they be brought to complete unity to let the world know that you sent me and have loved them" (John 17:23).

People realize that selfless love and unity are humanly impossible. When Christians show real love for each other and sacrifice their personal preferences for the sake of unity, others are convicted and attracted. No preaching compares with the impact of Christians loving each other.

To help you do the work of the kingdom. No one Christian has all the gifts necessary to spread the gospel, make mature disciples, help the needy, and combat Satan. God gave us different gifts to force us to depend on each other and work as a unit.

To worship with you. The Bible repeatedly exhorts us to worship together, not just to worship in private prayer. God is so great that He can be adequately worshipped only by a gathered community of His people. At first it may be hard to concentrate on praising God for any length of time.

To be Christ for you. It's important to be able to receive strength and love from God directly, because ultimately He is the source, not people. But God built us to need love "with skin on" sometimes. We need encouragement, affection, prayers, and practical help from others in Christ's name. God set up His kingdom so that none of us can survive or bear fruit without other Christians' help.

> Two are better than one,
>> because they have a good return for their work:
> If one falls down,
>> his friend can help him up.
> But pity the man who falls
>> and has no one to help him up! . . .
> Though one may be overpowered,
>> two can defend themselves.
> A cord of three strands is not quickly broken. (Ecclesiastes 4:9-10,12)

To keep you on track. On our own it's easy to be deluded about what the Bible says or what we should do. We start off relying on the Holy Spirit, but pretty soon we get overconfident of our discernment and wisdom. Prideful independence invites Satan to lead us astray.

> Whoever loves discipline loves knowledge,
>> but he who hates correction is stupid. (Proverbs 12:1)

Sharing your insights from the Bible with other believers will build them up and enable you to see nuances you hadn't noticed (Proverbs 27:17).

To help you surrender to God. Often, our reluctance to become involved with other believers stems less from self-confidence than from fear of being hurt. But God wants to deal with precisely this fear. *When* (not if) we are wounded, the pain drives us to our Father's arms. We will discover that He is able to heal the wound when we forgive, then we grow more willing to entrust control of our lives to Him. Choosing not to protect ourselves makes trusting God and loving people possible.

HOW SHOULD I RELATE TO OTHER CHRISTIANS?

Consider the "one another" passages:

- Wash one another's feet. (John 13:14)
- As I have loved you, so you must love one another. (John 13:34)
- Be devoted to one another in brotherly love. Honor one another above yourselves. (Romans 12:10)
- Live in harmony with one another. (Romans 12:16)
- Stop passing judgment on one another. (Romans 14:13)
- Have equal concern for each other. (1 Corinthians 12:25)
- Serve one another in love. (Galatians 5:13)
- Let us not become conceited, provoking and envying each other. (Galatians 5:26)
- Carry each other's burdens. (Galatians 6:2)

- Be patient, bearing with one another in love. (Ephesians 4:2)
- Be kind and compassionate to one another, forgiving each other, just as in Christ God forgave you. (Ephesians 4:32; compare Colossians 3:13)
- Submit to one another out of reverence for Christ. (Ephesians 5:21)
- Do not lie to each other. (Colossians 3:9)
- Let us consider how we may spur one another on toward love and good deeds. (Hebrews 10:24)
- Encourage one another. (Hebrews 10:25)
- Do not slander one another. (James 4:11)
- Don't grumble against each other. (James 5:9)
- Confess your sins to each other and pray for each other so that you may be healed. (James 5:16)
- Offer hospitality to one another without grumbling. (1 Peter 4:9)
- Clothe yourselves with humility toward one another. (1 Peter 5:5)

Finally,

Do nothing out of selfish ambition or vain conceit, but in humility consider others better than yourselves. Each of you should look not only to your own interests, but also to the interests of others. (Philippians 2:3-4)

The keys to unity are:

- Love selflessly
- Forgive generously

Ask God for help with these!

HOW DO I CHOOSE A SPIRITUALLY STRONG CHURCH?

You need a community that worships, that has mature Christians from whom you can seek counsel and correction, and that provides opportunities for you to learn what the Bible teaches.

Look for orthodox Christian faith. Churches vary in their specific beliefs, but here are a few core beliefs that all truly Christian churches share:

- God is a Trinity: Father, Son, and Holy Spirit are all fully God, yet distinct.
- Christ is fully God and fully man.
- Christ died for our sins, was buried, was raised from the dead on the third day, and ascended to the Father.
- The only way to be reconciled to God is by faith in Christ and His work on the cross.
- The Bible is the sufficient, trustworthy, authoritative source of truth about the faith.
- The church is the community of those who affirm these truths.

When you investigate a church, ask about these essentials. Listen to know whether the preaching promotes or undermines them.

Observe whether the church lives out its faith. Is accurate doctrine spurring people to love, compassion, obedience, and worship?

Make sure you can function within the structure. Churches differ in their methods of government (bishops, groups of elders, independent congregations). Understanding of the symbolic ceremonies (particularly baptism and communion) varies. Worship styles run from ancient chants to organs and hymns to guitars and drums, from deep reverence to relaxed freedom. Views on the ministry of lay people, especially women, also vary. Finally, some churches emphasize meeting children's needs, while others are good with teens, singles, couples, or older people. Don't join a church if you can't handle its style or if it fails to address a need you consider crucial.

You must be fed spiritually. Look for practical teaching, worship that draws you into the Father's presence, and small groups that let you get involved in others' lives.

Look for where you can serve best, not where you can best have your needs met. Your needs and preferences are important, but they aren't all-important. God may call you to a church that is not your "favorite flavor"—perhaps you have something to give there. Use all the resources of discernment to decide where to serve.

Meet with the leadership. Ask about their beliefs and their vision for the fellowship. Is that a vision you want to get behind?

Be sure the system of authority is biblical. It is possible to make a biblical case for either bishops, elders, or congregational voting. However, Jesus strongly warns against elevating a person to the level of absolute authority over others in the church or fellowship.

> You are not to be called "Rabbi," for you have only one Master and you are all brothers. And do not call anyone on earth "father," for you have one Father, and he is in heaven. Nor are you to be called "teacher," for you have one Teacher, the Christ. (Matthew 23:8-10)

Jesus is not splitting hairs about titles; He is forbidding an attitude of raising a person too high because it leads to domination, control, and idolatry. Some signs that a leader has unhealthy authority in a group are:

- Group members identify themselves more as "followers of so-and-so" than as "followers of Jesus Christ."
- People's need to be noticed and affirmed is used to control them.
- The leader is portrayed as one who is persecuted by outsiders or is working so hard for the group that it is shameful for you to work less than him or her.
- The threat of rejection or condemnation is used to control people's behavior.
- Discipline is extremely strict, and people are made to feel guilty if they fall short.
- The leader is portrayed as good, while you are bad.

- Everyone outside the group is unsaved, unholy. Group members are the only free and holy ones. People are threatened with losing their salvation, and even with disaster or death, if they leave the group.
- You are warned against seeking counsel or having friends outside the group because the outsiders are in delusion and evil.
- The group tries to control thoughts and feelings as well as behavior.
- All trouble or loss of control in the group is blamed on the Devil. Exorcisms may be common.
- Individuals' rights to choose are taken away in the interest of right behavior. The leader makes even daily decisions for the people.
- People are often accused of rebellion or lack of submission.

You may not find all these symptoms in a group, but think again if you notice a few. God invites people to be holy, but He never forces or shames them into obedience. You should be under authority in a loving body of believers, but be sure that the body has a healthy understanding of grace as well as holiness.

Once you join, be committed. If you've prayed, sought counsel, talked with the leadership, and decided that you can get behind the vision of this group, do it. When you uncover problems, be a part of the solution rather than leaving in disgust. Remember that every church is a hospital for sinners rather than a club for perfected saints.

STARTING A SMALL GROUP

One of those days Jesus went out to a mountainside to pray, and spent the night praying to God. When morning came, he called his disciples to him and chose twelve of them, whom he also designated apostles.

LUKE 6:12-13

WHY DO I NEED A SMALL GROUP?

Pages 133–135 describe why you need a Christian community. A large church can fill some of the following functions, but many require a small group of people who know you well and to whom you are committed:

- Sharing what the Lord has been teaching you, what you are thankful for, or some other gift to build up the body (1 Corinthians 14:26)
- Confessing your sins and praying for each other's healing (James 5:16)
- Learning to use your gifts for ministry in a safe environment

- Praying aloud together
- Encouraging each other in your daily struggles
- Seeking counsel
- Praying daily for others about needs you are familiar with
- Studying the Bible together
- Asking questions about the Bible or the faith
- Practicing sacrificial love in vulnerable situations

These require trust, intimate knowledge, and time. You will learn so much by watching how the group helps a member through a difficult struggle or how the group wrestles with a passage of Scripture. Your small group is your support system when you are:

- Sick and needing prayer or help with practical needs
- Facing a tough decision
- Struggling with a persistent sin
- Feeling like giving up

A loose association of friends who rarely meet all together is not as effective as a group that meets as a team frequently (ideally, once a week). You have to meet often if you are to:

- Know each other well
- Stay on top of what is going on in your lives
- Learn regularly from each other's insights on the Bible
- Act as partners in the gospel

WHAT DOES IT TAKE TO MAKE A SMALL GROUP WORK?

Define your purpose. Different groups have different emphases, levels of commitment, time requirements, and so on. A balanced group includes the following elements:

- Worship in song, praise, and thanksgiving
- Bible study, including application to your lives
- Sharing of personal issues (including confession and discussion if necessary)
- Prayer (especially for each other and your concerns)
- Outreach (some involvement with others, be it prayer for missionaries or unbelievers, pastoral care or service for others in your church, and so on)

Avoid pride. Pride is the chief killer of small groups. Privately rebuke those who use the group as a platform for showing off their knowledge. Limit those who talk too much. Encourage shy members to risk opening up. Don't let discussions degenerate into intellectual exercises; your goal is to let the Scriptures change your lives.

CAN I BE OPEN WITH THE MEMBERS OF MY SMALL GROUP?

The Puritans had a saying: "Have communion with few, be intimate with *one*. Deal justly with all, speak evil of none."[1] You need one or two Christian friends with whom you can confess any sin and discuss any concern. Then you need a small group of six to twelve Christian friends with whom you can share most things. Finally, you need a larger body of believers to worship and work with.

LIFE IN THE WORLD

If you should find yourself in the sight of God, and one said to you: "Look thither;" and God, on the other hand, should say: "It is not my will that you should look;" ask your own heart, what there is in all existing things, which would make it right for you to give that look contrary to the will of God. . . . I must confess that I ought not to oppose the will of God even to preserve the whole creation.

ST. ANSELM AND BOSO, *BIBLIOTHECA SACRA AND THEOLOGICAL REVIEW*

DISCERNING GOD'S WILL

*Do not conform any longer to the pattern of this world, but
be transformed by the renewing of your mind. Then you will
be able to test and approve what God's will is—his good,
pleasing and perfect will.*

ROMANS 12:2

A disciple wants to do what God wants, and this requires knowing
what He wants. We call this discerning God's will.

WHAT DO WE MEAN WHEN WE SPEAK OF "GOD'S WILL"?

God's sovereign will. The Bible says that God has a plan for
everything that happens in the universe: who will rule each nation
when, and what number will come up each time you roll dice.
This plan is *yet to be revealed*: We can't foresee God's future will
except insofar as He has revealed it through a biblical prophet. It
is also *certain*: Nothing can prevent God's sovereign will from
coming to pass.

God's general moral will. God has also revealed in the Bible
commands and principles to teach us how to live. The Bible
contains 100 percent of this will, and we are expected to discern
and obey it. Because we have choice, we can miss it through
ignorance or disobey it.

God's moral will has been fully revealed supernaturally and is recorded in the Bible. Its directives are general for all believers (Romans 2:18; 1 Thessalonians 4:3; 5:18).

God's individual will. Many Christians also believe that God has an "ideal, detailed life-plan uniquely designed for each person."[1] It includes His moral will, but it also includes such specifics as whom you should marry and where you should live and work this year. Those specifics are neither secret nor certain, yet they cannot be found in the Bible. They are revealed to each believer.

Other Christians believe that God does not have a detailed plan for what you should do at each step. Instead, He wants you to carefully evaluate the circumstances and your desires by biblical principles and wisdom, to pray for wisdom and guidance, and to be open to supernatural intervention if it comes. As long as your decision is within God's general moral will, He approves and will bless you.

Still others take a middle view: God leaves many decisions to your freedom (within His general will and wisdom) but has some specific plans, missions, or instructions for you.

Whichever view you take on the individual will, the common denominator in making godly decisions is learning *discernment*.

WHAT IS DISCERNMENT?

Discernment is the ability to perceive reality as it is. When God asked Solomon what he desired he answered not wealth, not victory over his enemies, but "a discerning heart to govern your people and to distinguish between right and wrong" (1 Kings 3:9).

Many of the biblical words for discernment (or good judgment) are related to verbs for tasting food.

> Solid food is for the mature, who by constant use have trained themselves to distinguish good from evil. (Hebrews 5:14)

So, discernment is the ability to taste right from wrong, good from evil (2 Samuel 19:35), truth from falsehood, the proper time and procedure from the wrong ones (Ecclesiastes 8:5). Such taste is trained through practice, just as a child learns to distinguish broccoli from ice cream and fresh food from spoiled.

WHAT GUIDANCE HAS GOD GIVEN ME TO HELP ME DISCERN?

God has provided you with eight areas of guidance:

- The Bible
- Personal desires
- Circumstances
- Mature counsel
- Common sense
- Results/experience
- Inner impressions
- Supernatural means (dreams, visions, and audible voices)

Your job is to weigh the input you get from your experiences and come up with a godly and wise decision. The more important the decision, the more effort you should put into weighing the input.

All true discernment must be rooted in the objective reality of the Bible. Specific feelings (inner impressions) about people or courses of action can be clues to truth, but we need to check them with objective reality. The first and foremost objective reality is the Bible, God's eternal Word (Psalm 119:66; Proverbs 2:1,9; 28:7; 2 Timothy 3:16-17).

God will never give you an instruction for a specific situation that contradicts the commands and values He expresses in His Word. Nor will He contradict the general spirit of the Word. If your feeling contradicts Scripture in any way, it is not from God.

Discernment must also be rooted in other objective reality. In addition to (but never instead of) the Bible, check *circumstances*:

- Factual evidence of the truth
- Careful research

For instance, if you feel you should move, look for objective, concrete reasons why God might want you to do that. In choosing a job, a house, or a college, do plenty of research. List the pros and cons of each option on a sheet of paper (Luke 14:28-32).

Evaluate the circumstances with wisdom. That is, use *common sense* and your own and others' past *experience*. "Wisdom is the power to see, and the inclination to choose, the best and highest goal, together with the surest means of attaining it."[2] God's wisdom is directed toward goals such as glorifying God, establishing His kingdom, and drawing you and others to be more like Christ. So, God's wisdom may sometimes contradict human wisdom, which promotes goals such as feeling good, getting ahead, and gaining people's approval. The Bible is your guide to heavenly goals and lawful means.

Pray for wisdom and guidance with reverence, humility, and faith. God promises to give wisdom to those who pray and have the attitudes of reverence, humility, and faith (Proverbs 9:10; 11:2; James 1:5-8).

Seek and accept correction.

Who can discern his errors?
Forgive my hidden faults. (Psalm 19:12)

The way of a fool seems right to him,
but a wise man listens to advice. (Proverbs 12:15)

Ask people with mature spiritual insight if they know any biblical principles that bear on your decision or on what you think God is saying. Ask people who have had relevant personal experiences if they learned anything that might be of value to you in your decision.[3]

Take personal desires into account. If your desires uphold God's goals of loving others and glorifying Him, and don't conflict with other things God wants you to do, then they are good guides. It is wise to eat what you enjoy, marry somebody you enjoy, and do a job you enjoy.

Be careful with inner impressions and revelations. These must always be verified by the Bible, wise counsel, and careful evaluation of objective reality. If God wants to give you a special instruction that seems objectively unwise (as He told Noah to build a huge boat miles from the sea), He will make that abundantly clear through supernatural means, and He will probably confirm it in several ways. He will never give you a special instruction that violates His eternal Word.

HOW CAN I ACQUIRE WISDOM AND DISCERNMENT?

Practice good personal discipline. Discernment requires daily training. That means daily time in Bible study to learn what God's will tastes like, daily time in listening prayer to learn what God's voice sounds like, and daily time holding your heart open to God's Word by meditating on it. It also means constancy in corporate worship, diligence in curbing your temper, faithfulness in your job, and so on. Together, these disciplines train you to act on truth and reality rather than emotions.

Practice making wise decisions. Discernment comes with daily practice in cultivating discipline, exercising discernment, and seeking correction.

Actively seek discernment (Proverbs 2:1-5).

Never trust the discernment of one whose words bring strife or confusion instead of healing. This is another kind of objective reality. If someone's information or counsel consistently cuts you or others up instead of convicting and building up, don't trust that counsel or believe that information (Proverbs 11:12; 12:18; 26:24-25; Matthew 7:15-16; James 3:13-18).

HOW DO THE PRINCIPLES OF DISCERNMENT APPLY TO MAKING WISE DECISIONS IN A SPECIFIC SITUATION?

Here are some questions to ask yourself when trying to decide what God wants or what is wise in a specific situation:

Is this decision in accord with the Word of God? That is, not individual verses taken out of context, but the whole spirit of the Word.

Is every part of this decision consistent with God's character? God will never tell you to do something that isn't loving, kind, courteous, and the rest of the traits in 1 Corinthians 13:4-7 and Galatians 5:22-23. For instance, He may tell you to confront someone about a grievance, but He would never tell you to confront in anger or condescension.

Is this decision wise?

Is all that this decision involves from the Lord? Our hearts tend to elaborate on what God says.

Is this decision confirmed by others in the body of Christ who are mature, respected Christians and who know me well? Listen to guidance given by leaders over you. If someone in authority corrects you, don't go looking for someone else who will support what you want to believe. If no mature Christian who is respected by many others in the body knows you well, take deliberate steps to do something about this. It is not wise to be out on your own, accountable to no one.

Is the word that led me to this decision persistent? If God is leading you in a direction, He won't stop bringing your attention to it. Take the time to check the guidance with objective reality and respected counselors, and keep your heart open for correction.

Is the guidance for this decision consistent with God's prior guidance to me? If after much prayer, study of the Scripture, counsel from respected believers who know you well, and objective confirmation, you've decided that God wants you to do something, stick to that decision. If someone then says to you, "God told me to tell you that you should do this other thing," don't believe them without incontrovertible evidence God has a new path for you.

WHAT DOES GOD SAY ABOUT CLAIMING "GOD TOLD ME . . ."?

> You shall not misuse the name of the LORD your God, for the LORD will not hold anyone guiltless who misuses his name. (Exodus 20:7)

> How long will this continue in the hearts of these lying prophets, who prophesy the delusions of their own minds? . . . I am against the prophets who wag their own tongues and yet declare, "The LORD declares." (Jeremiah 23:26,31)

Not every dream, feeling, or impulse is from God. Before you say, "The Lord told me . . . ," be sure you are right!

MAKING MORAL
DECISIONS

The one who sows to please his sinful nature, from that nature will reap destruction; the one who sows to please the Spirit, from the Spirit will reap eternal life.

GALATIANS 6:8

HOW DO I DECIDE WHAT IS RIGHT AND WRONG?

From Romans 14:1–15:3 and 1 Corinthians 8:1-11 we find important guidelines.

"Learn to distinguish between matters of command and matters of freedom."[1]

The Bible says some things are right in all cases—love, peace, joy, patience, kindness, goodness, faithfulness, gentleness, self-control, truthfulness, compassion, forgiveness, holiness, thankfulness, good stewardship of resources, and so on.

The Bible says some things are wrong in all cases—extramarital sex, lust, debauchery, idolatry, witchcraft, hatred, discord, jealousy, rage, selfish ambition, dissensions, factions, envy, drunkenness, greed, obscenity, foolish talk, coarse joking, covetousness, slander, malice, deceit, and so on.

Know your own limits. A place or activity might tempt one person to deceit or lust, while another might be unaffected. Be honest with yourself.

On disputable matters, form your own convictions. You are the one who will have to answer for your decisions before God! So ask yourself:

- Is there anything wrong with this activity? Will it lead me into any of the sins listed in the Bible?
- Is it profitable in some way?
- Will it build me or someone else up spiritually?
- Does it please me at someone else's expense?
- Can I thank God for this?
- Will this glorify God?
- Is it worth imitating?
- Does this follow Christ's example?

For instance, you might attend an activity just to show love to the non-Christian who invited you. As long as the activity doesn't tempt you to sin (know your limits), it may be the right thing to do. Christ went to parties with sinners for just this reason (Matthew 9:10-13; 11:19).

Obey your conscience. At any given point, what you believe in your heart or conscience to be sin, is sin for you (Romans 14:23). To choose against your conscience is to choose rebellion against God. It could also be a step toward learning to ignore your conscience. So don't let others pressure you into doing something you believe is wrong, even if you want to believe their arguments.

Allow other Christians the same freedom to choose. Although Christians differ in opinions and convictions, we must maintain acceptance and unity in relationships. Don't look down on a believer who does something you have concluded is wrong for you or who abstains from something you think is permissible.

Let love limit your liberty. The apostle Paul describes the "weaker brother" who sees you do something he thinks is wrong, but then is tempted to imitate you and violate his own conscience. These believers are weak in their convictions, biblical knowledge, conscience, and will—they don't have a firm grasp on biblical right and wrong, and they are easily swayed by others. You should voluntarily restrain your freedom when a weaker believer might be tempted to sin against his or her conscience.

Pharisees need not limit your liberty. Love does not mean you should restrain your freedom whenever someone complains. Jesus did not give in when the Pharisees complained. Pharisees are people who have strong convictions, are not tempted to act against their conscience, and are offended when you won't conform to their views.

Refuse to give in to their pressure to conform.

Graciously explain the reasons for your convictions when questioned.

Pursue peace and the Pharisee's good. If he or she rejects your efforts, leave that person alone.

Admonish others in the church to avoid Pharisaism, but don't backbite against specific Pharisees.

If a Pharisee begins to damage others or dishonor the Lord, *confront that person privately* in love, without name-calling or having a superior attitude.

Apply church discipline (Matthew 18:15-20) if private rebuke doesn't help.[2] If you aren't sure whether someone is a Pharisee or a weaker brother or sister, treat that person as the latter, and limit your liberty.

Look to Christ to model and enable your servanthood. It goes against the grain to limit your liberty for others and to resist getting mad at people who call you loose or legalistic. So immerse yourself in Christ's example and power. In following Jesus, Paul made a point of acting in any situation in the manner that glorified Christ (1 Corinthians 9:19-22). If that meant abstaining, he abstained. If it meant participating, he participated. Sin never makes Christ appear attractive to unbelievers, so he avoided that above all.

WHY DOES GOD CARE ABOUT THOUGHTS AND ACTIONS THAT AFFECT NO ONE BUT MYSELF?

Your actions always affect the body of Christ. "No man is an island, entire of itself; every man is a piece of the continent, a part of the main."[3]

When one soldier sinned, Joshua's entire army lost in battle (Joshua 7). This is true even more in the body of Christ: "If one part suffers, every part suffers with it; if one part is honored, every part rejoices with it" (1 Corinthians 12:26). If you are lazy about the time you spend with God, or indulge in sin, you lessen the spiritual strength and purity of the body to which you belong.

You don't own yourself. "You are not your own; you were bought at a price" (1 Corinthians 6:19-20). If you own your house, you can do what you like with it, but if you are renting, you have a responsibility to the owner. Because God owns you (having bought you out of a miserable bondage to death), you are responsible not to abuse His mind, heart, and body.

WHAT SHOULD I DO IF SOMEONE I KNOW IS PRACTICING SIN?

All people sin. But what if someone is practicing some sin as a habit?

> I have written you in my letter not to associate with sexually immoral people—not at all meaning the people of this world who are immoral, or the greedy and swindlers, or idolaters. In that case you would have to leave this world. But now I am writing you that you must not associate with anyone who calls himself a brother but is sexually immoral or greedy, an idolater or a slanderer, a drunkard or a swindler. With such a man do not even eat.
>
> What business is it of mine to judge those outside the church? Are you not to judge those inside? God will judge those outside. "Expel the wicked man from among you." (1 Corinthians 5:9-13)

Unbelievers. They are spiritually dead, blind, and imprisoned in "the dominion of darkness" (Colossians 1:13). You shouldn't be surprised if unbelievers practice sins. In order to be a light in their darkness, you can actively love them and be involved with them without participating in sinful activities.

Believers. Believers are responsible to their fellow Christians. Christians are jointly responsible to see that Christ's name is not dishonored among unbelievers because of the behavior of one who claims faith in Him. So, you should confront your brother or sister privately. If that person repents, forgive him or her completely. If you have to confront that person in the same sin repeatedly, but you have evidence that he or she is honestly struggling with it, then repeatedly forgive that individual (Luke 17:3-4). Don't withhold love and support from someone who still falls in the struggle to resist temptation.

However, if a person professes repentance only verbally, or not at all, and seems to have no intention of seeking God's strength to change, then confront him or her with a few other Christians. If that fails, bring the matter to your pastor (Matthew 18:15-17).

New believers. It takes time for new believers to realize sinful habits and begin to change, so show them Christlike love. Through Scripture and example, teach the outlook on life and the values of a Christian. As a new believer comes to understand commitment and sacrifice, the reasons for not doing a certain sin will become obvious. If a new believer is a member of your fellowship for a long period of time and you observe no change, then that person moves into the category of believers and should be confronted.

DEALING WITH EMOTIONS

Above all else, guard your heart, for it is the wellspring of life.

PROVERBS 4:23

ARE STRONG EMOTIONS GOOD OR BAD?

Emotions are often rooted in physical responses. An adrenaline rush that causes a pounding heart and a flushed face is your body's response to a threat. A hormone flood is a natural response to the proximity of the opposite sex. People of different ages and body types have different levels of physical responses, but there is no sin in having strong ones.

An emotion is an interpretation of the circumstances, based on what you believe deep down. When someone pushes you from behind and you experience an adrenaline rush, you automatically interpret the physical feeling as anger or fear, depending on what kind of threat you think the push is. When someone hurts you, you interpret the situation as a thwarting of desires or a denial of essential needs, and you accordingly feel mild or deep disappointment, anger, or bitterness.

Emotions are messages. If you feel angry or nervous when your spouse presses you to talk, your heart may be telling you,

"I am afraid to be vulnerable to this person; I am afraid he will lose respect if he knows the real me; I am afraid that he will use my secrets to manipulate me; I don't trust God to take care of my need for respect and to protect me from a controlling husband; I have never forgiven my father and mother for trying to control me." This extremely useful information tells you about your relationships with God, your spouse, and your parents.

The moral issue is what you do with the feeling. The feeling is what you really believe. Ask yourself: Is this belief true? Do I need to renew my mind in God's truth (Romans 12:1-2)? How will I respond?

Listen to your feelings, but act (use your will) on what you know (in your mind) is true.

SHOULD I TRUST MY FEELINGS OF GUILT?

Guilt is a feeling of having violated your inner code of conduct.[1]

Guilt is necessary for repentance. Repentance requires that we are convicted that we are wrong and God is right. Jesus' death can do nothing for us until we recognize that we are guilty.

Your inner code may be inaccurate. Satan sometimes tries to discourage believers by setting an impossible standard, and then condemning us when we fail. You never *feel* forgiven because there is no real guilt and God is not condemning you. Likewise, you can set unrealistic standards for yourself (I must never let my child be hurt; I must never pass up a chance to give to someone else; I must never be angry) or learn them from our parents.

On the other hand, you can silence your conscience by repeatedly ignoring it when it tells you not to do something. Or it may approve an action because society or family has taught you to think it is okay.

Evaluate your conscience by truth: God's Word. If you feel guilty about an action but the Bible does not condemn it, then don't condemn yourself. If you feel guilty for having failed to meet a biblical standard, confess and receive forgiveness. Don't insult Christ by refusing to accept forgiveness after His sacrifice has been applied to your sin. God doesn't expect you to be utterly holy already; it is only your pride that demands perfection of you. In fact, humility about your own frailty is one of the things God most wants you to learn.

If you don't feel guilty about an action but God's Word forbids it, then don't do it. God will never contradict Himself, no matter what you feel.

HOW CAN I BE ANGRY WITHOUT SINNING?

Sinful anger is when you desire the other person to suffer for what he has done. It turns to bitterness when you refuse to forgive.

You avoid sin by thinking, "You have frustrated my desires and cost me something. I feel the cost deeply. But because I know that God is taking care of my needs, I am willing to bear this without desiring you to suffer. Rather, I desire that you be blessed."

If someone smashes your car, it is justice to expect him to pay for the repairs. But choosing forgiveness rather than nursing anger means that you will not wish the person ill, even though you must bear the frustration of the experience.

COPING WITH SUFFERING

We also rejoice in our sufferings, because we know that suffering produces perseverance; perseverance, character; and character, hope.

ROMANS 5:3-4

HOW CAN A LOVING GOD LET PEOPLE SUFFER?

God doesn't enjoy seeing people suffer, but He does use suffering for good purposes:

To judge sin in general. God made a world in which actions have consequences. He gave humans the dignity of affecting what would happen. When Adam sinned, he subjected his whole earthly domain to natural diseases, disasters, and death. When generations of sinners make billions of selfish, destructive choices, they add political oppression, cruelty, poverty, war, and a host of other evils.

God created a world in which descendants would inherit the benefits of their ancestors' wisdom and kindness; we turned it into a world in which children inherit genetic flaws, poverty, pollution, and abusive behavior. God allows the "innocent" to suffer because we reap what we have sown. In this way, God remains faithful to the just, loving laws He laid down at Creation.

To judge sin in specific. God sometimes sends disaster on a nation because of its repeated sin, a heart attack on a person who has been arrogantly striving, financial ruin on someone who has been dishonest, or even illness on a person who has dishonored the Lord's Supper (1 Corinthians 11:28-30). However, we should not assume nation or individual is suffering because of some specific sin.

To strengthen our faith. Suffering is one of the best ways of conforming us to Jesus' likeness (Romans 5:3-4; 8:28-29; James 1:2-4).

To demonstrate that our faith is genuine. Satan claimed that Job served God out of self-interest, not love. Satan said Job would reject God if his earthly blessings were taken away (Job 2:3-5). This was a serious attack on God's integrity (God doesn't buy people's loyalty) and Job's. So, God let Satan tempt Job to betray God in order to vindicate both Job and Himself. By enduring suffering without renouncing God, we prove to all forces of darkness and light, as well as to people on earth, that God is worthy of love even though He doesn't buy it with blessings. We also prove that we are giving love freely, not selling it to buy comfort.

To remind us of eternity. It's easy to feel proud that we are making it on our own when things are going well, but suffering can jar us into realizing that we are dependent upon God. It can remind us that earthly comfort is temporary, but what matters is eternity.

To make us more human. Suffering is part of life. When you have suffered, you grow more vulnerable, more richly able to enjoy people and pleasure, more able to reach out with compassion.

To spread the gospel. People are attracted to Christ when they see a believer handling crises with grace and confidence in God.

To show that Satan's worst won't stop God. Satan hates true believers, so "everyone who wants to live a godly life in Christ Jesus will be persecuted" (2 Timothy 3:12). But when God turns Satan's worst into triumph for the gospel, proof of someone's faith, or some other unexpected good, God proves that He is supremely powerful, wise, and good. That is the central issue of the war between God and Satan.

To unite us with Christ. God showed His compassion for us by entering into our suffering as a man. Christ drew into Himself all the suffering of every person, and He suffers with every sufferer. When we suffer, especially for others, we identify ourselves with the Lord and know Him more intimately. The resulting depth of maturity and oneness with Christ is profound.

HOW CAN I DEAL WITH MY OWN SUFFERING?

Know that God will use it for good. God can use your suffering for one or more of the purposes just discussed, or for some other good purpose you can't envision (Romans 8:28).

Seek good uses. Pray that your attitude amid suffering will glorify God and draw others to Christ. Seize the opportunity to learn compassion so that you can comfort others when they are similarly afflicted (2 Corinthians 1:3-7). Let it drive you to depend on God and grow in faith. Rejoice that Satan's claim (that sufferers will renounce God) is being proven empty before all the powers of the universe.

Get support. Persist in prayer, Bible reading, and fellowship with other believers. Seek others to pray with and for you. Talk out your feelings, fears, doubts, and hopes with people you trust.

Don't rationalize. Don't make up reasons why God has allowed a tragedy (such as, "God killed my son in order to teach me something"). Accept not knowing why, rather than inventing reasons to feel better.

Focus on good. Pay close attention to the good people and the pleasures in your life, and praise God for them.

WHAT SHOULD I DO WHEN GOD SEEMS FAR AWAY?

Examine your feelings and beliefs. God sometimes seems distant because of feelings or false beliefs about Him.

Are you angry at God about something that has happened? If so, tell Him how you feel. God allows us to suffer the consequences of our own mistakes and even to suffer innocently for others' errors (a car crash, war, and so on) and natural disasters. This is part of reality. God won't get mad if you express your feelings to Him. After you've expressed your feelings, remind yourself of the truth about God: He loves you, and He is totally just, wise, and good.

Are you afraid of God? Immerse yourself in Scriptures that remind you that He is a loving, forgiving Father, and that Jesus has satisfied the just demands of His wrath. He is not angry at you, and He welcomes you into His presence. If your earthly father was a frightening person, it can be hard not to project that character onto God. If so, go through the steps of forgiving your father (see pages 174–175). Ask God to help you see Him as He really is, not as you imagine Him.

Are you feeling guilty? Evaluate your feelings by biblical standards. If you aren't really guilty of a certain sin, let go of the feeling. If you are guilty, confess.

Confess known sin. Unconfessed sin is the one thing that separates you from sensing God's nearness. Sin doesn't make you lose your salvation, but it does block you from experiencing God's presence and having your prayers answered. Don't go on a morbid hunt for every past or present fault of thought or deed. Instead, examine your life for clear bitterness toward someone, immorality, divisiveness, wrong desire, or idolatry.

Check your needs and your desires. You may be depressed because people or circumstances frustrate your desire for respect (status, recognition) or love (affection, attention). Your pride may be wounded. Holding these frustrations against God makes it difficult to approach Him. Or feeling worthless and hurt may make you want to close in on yourself. Meditating on the Psalms and getting others to pray and talk with you can help.

Take care of your body. Lack of sleep, exercise, and healthy food feed depression and sap your spiritual life.

Give. God dwells with the lowly, the hurting, and the outcast (Isaiah 57:15, and notice in the Gospels where Jesus spends His time). If you want to be where God is, reach out to others.

Remember you are not unique. The psalmists (Psalm 42) and Christians of every age have experienced what is called "the dark night of the soul" when God seems absent. God uses this experience to teach us to depend not on feelings of His presence but on unshakable faith. Let the feeling of absence drive you to prayer and praise, not keep you from them. Read classics on prayer and devotion to reignite the fire in your heart.

Go where you are more likely to experience God. Keep attending worship services, praying with friends, and reading the Bible.

Be patient. Wait, wait, and wait some more. Where is God when you are hurting? If you wait long enough you will find out that He is right there, hurting with you all along.

Respond to opportunities. Open yourself to God in worship. Keep setting aside your doubts that God will ever be present again. Respond positively to even glimpses of His presence.

HOW CAN I HELP SOMEONE ELSE WHO IS SUFFERING?

Don't give pat answers. People often ask, "Why?" but unless God gives you a direct revelation, you don't know for sure. Job's friends were convinced they knew why he was suffering, but their clichés missed the mark. They also revealed a lack of sensitivity to Job's feelings. If God wants to teach someone through suffering, you will only get in the way if you reduce the painful, experiential lesson to a trite sentence or single Bible verse.

Be present. Your silent presence is often the best way to show you care.

Use discernment. One person might benefit from hearing you tell jokes, another from chatting about some interesting topic, another from telling you how angry or frightened he is, another from having you hold her while she cries. Ask God to show you what is needed and to give you the courage to do it.

Don't argue. Hurting people often say outrageous things. Give them a chance to vent their feelings, even if they insult God. He won't fall off His throne; He can defend Himself. Wait until the feelings are vented and the person is calm to discuss rationally what has been said.

RELATING TO OTHERS

Let us not become weary in doing good, for at the proper time we will reap a harvest if we do not give up.

GALATIANS 6:9

HOW DOES GOD WANT ME TO TREAT PEOPLE IN GENERAL?

God has specific instructions for relating to spouses, parents, children, masters, servants, fellow Christians, and unbelievers. But many of His commands apply to all relationships.

Love. Love is seeking the other person's highest good, even if it costs you a great deal. Our model is Christ, who poured out His life for people who did not love Him back. We are commanded to love fellow Christians, enemies, whomever we encounter (Luke 6:27-38; 10:25-37).

Love is patient [does not retaliate when hurt], love is kind. It does not envy, it does not boast, it is not proud. It is not rude, it is not self-seeking, it is not easily angered, it keeps no record of wrongs. Love does not delight in evil but rejoices with the truth. It always protects, always trusts, always hopes, always perseveres. (1 Corinthians 13:4-7)

Love is an act of will, not a feeling, so you can choose to love someone even when you don't feel affection for them. Ask yourself, "If I cared deeply about this person, what would I do?" When you've answered that, do it. Persistently acting in love fosters loving feelings in us, whereas failing to act in love hinders loving feelings. Paying the cost of putting others' interests first is possible because we know that God is taking care of our needs (Luke 12:22-34) and that He has paid the ultimate cost.

Forgiveness.

> If you forgive men when they sin against you, your heavenly Father will also forgive you. But if you do not forgive men their sins, your Father will not forgive your sins. (Matthew 6:14-15)

Holding bitterness in your heart against someone blocks you from receiving God's forgiveness. We are judged by whatever standard we use to measure others (Matthew 7:1-2). So if you find it difficult to forgive someone, follow these steps:

Take your grief to God, and describe to Him exactly how you feel. The psalmists used word pictures (I feel like a crushed bag, like I'm smothering, like I've been stabbed) to express their anger and grief.

Turn from feelings to facts. Remind yourself that God fully loves and respects you, so your self-worth doesn't rest on a person's response to you. Memorize and recite relevant Scripture to yourself. That may help you focus on truth rather than on feelings.

Ask God for the strength to forgive, let go of the hurt, and trust again. Ask Him to remember that although your desires have been thwarted and your pride bruised, your real needs are intact. If you can, thank God for taking your pride down a notch.

Choose to forgive as an act of your will. You may have to choose forgiveness repeatedly while the pain takes time to heal. The process goes faster if you pray blessings for the person and treat him or her with love every chance you get.

Discuss the issue with a friend, if it's important. Forgiving doesn't mean that the person wasn't wrong. It doesn't mean shielding the person from lawful punishment. Forgiving simply means choosing to let go of bitterness and the desire for revenge and to seek the other's highest good.

Humility. We all tend to act as though one person in the world (self) should take precedence over all others. Humility is ceasing to compete for top billing. Humility isn't putting yourself down; it is ceasing to be preoccupied with yourself at all. Humble people take a genuine interest in others' needs, feelings, and opinions. They know God loves and values them, so they don't have to prove their value to themselves or others (John 13:3-5).

FORMING GOOD FRIENDSHIPS

Two are better than one, because they have a good return
for their work: If one falls down, his friend can help him up.
But pity the man who falls and has no one to help him up!

ECCLESIASTES 4:9-10

HOW CAN I BE A GOOD FRIEND?

Focus on serving, not on having your needs met. All people need to know that they are deeply and unconditionally loved just as they are, and that they are engaged in a truly important task for which they are competent. That is, we need love because of who we are and respect because we matter. Because we generally assume that only other people can meet those needs, we tend to go into relationships with the intent of having our needs met. When people fail us, we become angry, even bitter.

However, God is the only One who can meet those deep needs. By giving up His Son to deliver us from misery and death, God demonstrated that He loves us unconditionally (Romans 5:5-8; 8:31-39). By commissioning us as His agents to restore His kingdom on earth, God assured us that we matter, and through His Holy Spirit He enables us not to fail in this mission. People are meant to help us feel His love and valuing, and it is okay to *desire* them to do so. But if we claim to *need* their love and respect, that shows self-centeredness, pride, and failure to trust God.

So, instead of trying to manipulate others into fulfilling our desires, we should focus on being God's instrument to help them feel His love and valuing. We are able to glorify God by putting others first because we are secure that our needs are met in Him.

Be vulnerable. Having all your needs met in Christ doesn't mean you can do without intimate relationships. It's easy to be the strong one who listens to the other person's problems and gives counsel, comfort, and forgiveness. This makes you feel superior and needed, and you keep yourself from getting hurt badly.

It's tough to let down your mask of competence and your self-protective walls, and let others see your pains and faults. They may condescend, tell other people your secrets, fail to really understand, lose respect, condemn, or reject.

Jesus didn't have to become vulnerable to despisers and rejecters, but He did (Isaiah 53:3). One of His closest friends betrayed Him to death. The rest let Him down when He needed their support (Mark 14:32-52,66-72). They never really understood Him.

But Jesus knew that vulnerability was worth the risk. For Him, the goal was to teach His friends what real love and trust—bearing each other's burdens—meant. You can't teach a fearful person to trust by being afraid to trust that person. For us, the goal also includes escaping from our own prison of loneliness. Even though no one can understand us fully and love us perfectly, a friend can be a real help.

Jesus had the courage to risk betrayal because His ultimate trust was in God. He knew that people's rejection couldn't destroy Him because He was accepted by the One who mattered the most. His self-worth came from His Father.

Yet though Jesus didn't need people for His self-worth, He let Himself desire to feel the Father's love and respect through His friends. He let Himself feel hurt by them. We, who are far less holy and strong than He, should find no shame in admitting to someone, "Your love and respect matter deeply to me."

Be available, loyal, honest, selfless (Proverbs 17:17; 18:24; 27:6,17).

Don't expect perfection. If you expect your friends to fail in love, availability, loyalty, and honesty, then you won't be crushed when they fail. Demanding perfection from others is selfish and unrealistic. Remember: You aren't a perfect friend either. Your job is to hold your heart open, knowing that at times you will be hurt.

Share biblical truth. Besides sharing your feelings, *share* what God is teaching you through circumstances, prayer, and the Bible. This is a great way to get excited about Bible study. It also grounds your friendship in something deeper than feelings. Learn to tell your friend what you are learning and to *listen* to him or her. The goal of sharing and listening is to grow close to God and each other, not to impress each other with your knowledge.

Confess your sins to each other (James 5:16). This should lead not to judgment or condoning, but to prayer and support to turn away from sin.

Hold each other accountable. Encourage each other to apply what you've learned from God. Keep up with how each of you is doing. Pray for each other about your struggles to obey God. Let your friend ask you how your prayer and meditation on Scripture are going. Be honest with each other.

WHAT IF A FRIEND LETS ME DOWN?

It's inevitable that friends will let us down. Follow the steps for forgiveness on pages 174–175.

CAN I HAVE NON-CHRISTIAN FRIENDS?

Non-Christians probably can't be your closest friends, as they can't share in the most important part of your life. Your attitudes, motives, and activities will be foreign to them. Yet you definitely should love, spend time with, talk at some depth with, be available and loyal to, and be somewhat vulnerable with—in short, be friends with—non-Christians. Nearly everyone who comes to Christ does so partly because of a Christian friend. So if you have no unbelieving friends, your effectiveness as Jesus' ambassador will be small.

WHAT SHOULD I DO IF A FRIEND ASKS ME TO DO SOMETHING I THINK IS WRONG?

When Paul says, "Everything that does not come from faith is sin" (Romans 14:23), he means that it is wrong to do anything you believe is wrong, even if someone else disagrees. A real friend won't pressure you into doing something that violates your conscience. Anyone who would dissolve a friendship if you refuse to go along with something is using you—exploiting your need for affirmation, affection, and belonging. Peter's answer to the Jewish authorities applies equally to friends who ask you to violate your conscience: "We must obey God rather than men!" (Acts 5:29). Paul's refusal to go along with his critics also applies.

> Am I now trying to win the approval of men, or of God? Or am I trying to please men? If I were still trying to please men, I would not be a servant of Christ. (Galatians 1:10)

THINKING ABOUT DATING

I urge you, brothers, in view of God's mercy, to offer your bodies as living sacrifices, holy and pleasing to God—this is your spiritual act of worship. Do not conform any longer to the pattern of this world, but be transformed by the renewing of your mind.

ROMANS 12:1-2

WHAT SHOULD BE MY ATTITUDE ABOUT DATING?[1]

Some Christians think that dating unbelievers is always foolish, because dating can lead to marriage and because unbelievers are likely to have lower moral standards than God wants you to have.

Good reasons for a date:

- To develop social skills (communication, sensitivity, and so on)
- To have a good time
- To enjoy another person's whole personality
- To enjoy being genuinely accepted by someone
- To grow in Christ through fellowship with another believer

Bad reasons for a date:

- To impress the date or other people
- To obtain sexual gratification
- To build up your ego
- To get the other person to meet your needs

Good questions to govern behavior:

- Is my motive to satisfy myself or honor this person?
- Am I treating this person as a precious creature of God with feelings and an eternal destiny?
- Does this relationship help me know myself and Christ better?
- Does this person encourage me to obey God?
- Am I doing this because of pressure from parents, friends, or my date?
- Am I trying to get this person to meet needs that God should meet?

Women's responsibilities. Women are often more verbal than men. You can contribute to your date's growth by making it safe for him to communicate (for instance, not manipulating him with what you learn about him), being open yourself, listening, and asking good questions.

Men's responsibilities. Assume responsibility for spiritual leadership without being overbearing. Keep your date's welfare in mind. Plan your time together, and don't get your date into compromising or uncomfortable situations.

Learn to communicate with words rather than touch. Decide to risk exposing your real thoughts and feelings. Open up slowly, to see whether you can trust this woman. Don't get involved with someone you can't trust with your private thoughts, even though you find her attractive.

Restrain your desire to conquer. Don't make a woman think you are more emotionally committed than you really are. Don't use her need for love against her.

STAYING SEXUALLY PURE

Do you not know that your body is a temple of the Holy Spirit, who is in you, whom you have received from God? You are not your own; you were bought at a price. Therefore honor God with your body.

1 CORINTHIANS 6:19-20

WHAT DOES THE BIBLE SAY ABOUT SEX?

It's good. God created human beings to be sexual (Genesis 1:27). He designed us for physical attraction and pleasure. The one-flesh relationship between husband and wife was always intended to be physical as well as spiritual. Sex releases biological tension and expresses one's acceptance of and willing interdependence with another person. Marital sex should be joyful.

> May your fountain be blessed,
>> and may you rejoice in the wife of your youth.
> A loving doe, a graceful deer—
>> may her breasts satisfy you always,
>> may you ever be captivated by her love. (Proverbs 5:18-19)

The Fall has marred sex. Several aspects of sin have corrupted human sexuality. Pride and mutual fear have driven a wedge between men and women. No longer trusting God to meet their needs, people use sex to manipulate each other into giving love and respect. The normal physical desire is inflamed by association with ego desires. Thus, sex becomes a tool, a weapon, an obsession.

Sex is for married couples only. First Corinthians 6:9-20 and other passages make it clear that premarital sex is as damaging as cheating on a spouse. Sex is an expression of a lifelong commitment.

Lust is as wrong as acting it out. Sins of the heart are just as harmful to you and as anti-God as active sins. But remember, there is a difference between lust and attraction. It's normal to notice other people's bodies and personalities, and even to have a physical reaction to someone's presence. It's normal to feel tempted to lust. Temptation becomes sin when you dwell on the desire or fantasize about it.

Desiring your mate is not lust. Lust is illicit desire. Because God made you to desire your mate, that desire is as good as wanting to sleep each night and eat each day. In fact, God commands married couples to fulfill each other sexually (1 Corinthians 7:3-5).

It is possible, however, to desire your mate wrongly. God says that holiness and honor should govern marital sex (1 Thessalonians 4:3-5). You dishonor your spouse if you demand sexual acts that he or she finds degrading or if you demand sex when he or she feels unable. Demanding and resenting are both sins. If your spouse refuses, it is a sign that you need (possibly with a counselor present) to talk out the root of the problem.

WHAT IS WRONG WITH HAVING SEX OUTSIDE OF MARRIAGE?

God doesn't make rules arbitrarily. Sexual purity is hard to maintain not because it is unnatural, but because sin has marred our natures and corrupted our sex drives.

Wrong motives. Sexual intercourse is intended to express oneness between husband and wife, in which each gives himself or herself voluntarily and wholly to the other. Sex for any other reason is manipulating another person to meet prideful and selfish goals. Examples of wrong motives for sex include:

- To repay or secure a favor
- To prove one's ability to conquer someone
- To feel intimate (loved, accepted) when you fear verbal communication
- To buy affection or loyalty
- To feel admired by or important to someone
- To overcome feelings of inferiority
- To drown feelings of anxiety or tension
- To control the other person emotionally
- To win respect from other people
- To obtain pleasure for self[1]

Destructive effects.

Everything you do with your body affects your spirit. Your body and spirit know that sexual intercourse signifies one-flesh commitment (1 Corinthians 6:12-20). When you try to perform the act without the meaning, your spirit feels united-but-not-united with the other person, confused, lost. Every time you do this, you weaken your ability to bond with a marriage partner later. You'll find yourself comparing him or her to previous sexual partners or just unable to give yourself totally.

Extramarital sex insults God's Spirit and so separates you from Him. Your prayers go unanswered, your faith crumbles, everything you try to do for God proves empty even if it looks good for a while. Christ redeemed and bought your body as well as your soul. Your body is not yours to do with as you please.

A relationship based on mutual exploitation for pleasure will eventually end. You will feel rejected and used. You'll find your craving for love and respect is even worse. If you bury the hurt under pride ("It doesn't matter to me"), you deaden your ability to feel, face reality, and relate to either God or people.

"Sex prevents other aspects of the relationship from developing."[2] You may struggle to learn to communicate, to work things out, to trust each other, if you depend on sex to bind your relationship together.

You'll infect your relationship with fear, mistrust, and guilt. Even if you don't want to accept God's Law, your heart does, and it will plague you. If you do eventually marry, those feelings of fear, mistrust, and guilt will follow. You'll feel vaguely unclean having sex with your spouse. And when the romance fades, you may be tempted to suspect him or her of unfaithfulness. After all, if your spouse couldn't control his or her appetites before marriage, why should you trust that person in marriage?

You may deceive yourself into thinking you're in love. Infatuation can go on for three to five years. You may get married and then find out the attraction was only physical.

WHAT ABOUT SEXUAL CONTACT SHORT OF CONSUMMATION?

In a healthy relationship, physical intimacy grows gradually as personal commitment grows: eye to eye, hand to hand, hand to shoulder, hand to waist, hand to face, mouth to mouth, hand to body, and so on. Physical contact is designed to prepare the body and spirit for consummation. The progression has enormous energy of its own. It is wise to halt it before it starts to arouse lust because:

- It is sin to purposely incite another person to lust.
- Arousing the body deeply without satisfying it produces extreme tension, which can shatter the relationship in an emotional blowup.
- Physical intimacy on the brink of intercourse can affect the spirit just as consummation does.

WHAT CAN I DO ABOUT SEXUAL TEMPTATION?

Beating yourself with guilt won't help. Confession, prayer, and support from other Christians will. Most importantly, get your needs met from God, and work things out with your spouse, if you have one.

WHAT CAN I DO IF I'VE ALREADY FALLEN?

No sin is too big for God to forgive and cleanse you from. If you feel unable to find forgiveness, try these steps:[3]

Complete repentance. Ask God to remind you of everything in your past that has violated His commands in this area. Write a list, or tell someone you trust who won't be tempted to sin by hearing your story. (Choose someone mature in faith. You don't need to describe details.) Then pray about your list, asking God to forgive you, and telling Him that you never want to fall prey in this area again. Ask Him to cleanse your mind and heart of the confusion, fear of intimacy, feelings of dirtiness, or any other bad effects. Thank Him for forgiving, cleansing, and freeing you. If it helps, have your friend say out loud that you are forgiven. Tear up your list.

Complete immersion. During the next weeks, immerse yourself in biblical passages that speak of God's mercy, forgiveness, and love (such as Psalm 103:12; Isaiah 43:12; Hebrews 9:13-14). This will help your heart and mind come to terms with God's forgiveness.

WHAT ARE SOME IMPORTANT DIFFERENCES BETWEEN MEN AND WOMEN?

Understanding the differences between men and women can help you overcome frustrations and communication barriers. The following are helpful generalizations (exceptions are common):

- Menstruation, lactation, and pregnancy all involve hormones that affect a woman's emotional state.
- Female physiology is "more complex and vulnerable"[4] than male. Severe shocks affect a woman's biochemistry, and hence her emotions, more easily than a man's.

- Women tend to be more future-oriented. They value "stability, security, and enduring human relationships" more than men. This may be due to the reproductive bent of a woman's body.

- Similarly, women tend to invest more in their homes (the nest) and family, while men focus on the outer world. This produces balance when the friction is dealt with.

- Men tend to crave respect more than love, while women crave love more than respect (Ephesians 5:33).

- Men approach games and work more competitively. Men seek conquest, while women seek relationship. Broadly generalizing, men are more goal- and task-oriented, while women are more process- and experience-oriented.

- Men are more quickly aroused sexually than women. Men are more visually oriented, while women respond more to touch. For men, the tension of desire is more acutely physical. Women crave sex more as an expression of love. Personal intimacy, romance, caring, respect, admiration—these emotional factors are more important to a woman's sexual interest; men are more easily aroused just by the sight of the body. These facts explain why women will use sex to buy affection, while men will use affection to buy sex. Understanding these differences also explains why a little romance and a lot of touching outside the bed improve a woman's interest enormously.

HONORING GOD IN MARRIAGE

*Each one of you also must love his wife as he loves himself,
and the wife must respect her husband.*

EPHESIANS 5:33

HOW DOES THE BIBLE DESCRIBE A CHRISTIAN MARRIAGE?
One flesh.

> It is not good for the man to be alone. I will make a helper suitable for him. (Genesis 2:18)

> For this reason a man will leave his father and mother and be united to his wife, and they will become one flesh. (Genesis 2:24)

Husband and wife are the closest possible unity, a single organism. They don't function as separate individuals, each trying to fulfill himself or herself. In all things, they should "submit to one another out of reverence for Christ" (Ephesians 5:21).

"Helper" is an honorable title; God calls Himself our Helper

(Psalm 10:14; 118:7). The wife is an indispensable partner in the couple's joint mission, perfectly designed to complement her husband's gifts and compensate for his limitations. She should be his closest friend and confidante, and he hers.

Their unity is so profound that it is a visible picture of Christ's unity with the church (Ephesians 5:21-23).

WHAT SHOULD I LOOK FOR IN A SPOUSE?

Believers must marry only believers. This is the Bible's only absolute command on this subject (1 Corinthians 7:39; 2 Corinthians 6:14-16). It is wrong and very unwise to choose a partner who is loyal to anything other than Jesus Christ. You will regret choosing a spouse who does not share your commitment. Do not put "love" for a person before loving obedience to your King.

Choose someone who is morally and spiritually mature. You want the best possible partnership for spreading God's kingdom. Proverbs 31:10-31 lists traits of an excellent or noble wife. Galatians 5:22-23, Ephesians 4:20-32, and Colossians 3:12-17 describe a godly man or woman.

Can you submit to and love this person? Ephesians 5:21-33 describes the way a Christian couple should relate. Ask yourself, "Do I respect this man enough to submit to him even when I disagree? Is this a man who can love me sacrificially?" Or, "Is this a woman I can love the way Christ loves the church? Will this woman be able to put me ahead of her other interests?" Remember, you are going to have to trust this person completely.

Seek and accept the counsel of your parents and mature believers who know you well.

Are you compatible? Discuss with your intended mate finances, employment, personal goals, birth control, child rearing, and so on. Consider age, education, personality traits, hobbies, and family background. Remember, you are going to have to come to agreement about a wide range of issues.

HOW SHOULD I TREAT MY SPOUSE?
Like Christ and His body. All of the guidelines on fellowships, relationships, and friendships apply above all to you and your spouse. In addition, wives are to treat their husbands as they would treat Christ, and husbands are to treat their wives as Christ treats the church:

> Wives, submit to your husbands as to the Lord. For the husband is the head of the wife as Christ is the head of the church, his body, of which he is the Savior. Now as the church submits to Christ, so also wives should submit to their husbands in everything.
>
> Husbands, love your wives, just as Christ loved the church and gave himself up for her to make her holy, cleansing her by the washing with water through the word, and to present her to himself as a radiant church, without stain or wrinkle or any other blemish, but holy and blameless. In this same way, husbands ought to love their wives as their own bodies. He who loves his wife loves himself. After all, no one ever hated his own body, but he feeds and cares for it, just as Christ does the church—for we are members of his body. "For this reason a man will leave his father and mother and be united to his wife, and the two will

become one flesh." This is a profound mystery—but I am talk-ing about Christ and the church. However, each one of you also must love his wife as he loves himself, and the wife must respect her husband. (Ephesians 5:22-33)

Love is a commitment. Your unity and love are a commitment even when you feel angry or unattracted. Knowing that each of you is committed—regardless of failure, aging, or disagreement—enables you to feel secure when you hit rocky times. If the commit-ment is only as strong as your feelings, then you will have to constantly walk on eggshells and sweep things under the rug to maintain the marriage.

You are responsible to treat your spouse according to all of God's commands, even if he or she doesn't recognize or obey those commands. This is tough if you've married an unbeliever or some-one with immature or nominal faith, but you are still responsible for your actions.

Communication is essential. In order to function as a unit, you *must* make talking a priority. If you are busy, you must sched-ule a few hours each week just to talk with each other. Talk about:

- With whom have you been dealing during the week?
- Do you have good relationships with these people?
- What are your major responsibilities each day?
- Are you able to handle them?
- Do you need wisdom and encouragement for dealing with a relationship or a responsibility?
- Do you have large or small decisions to make as a couple?

Avoid or repent of these barriers to communication:

- The attitude that some sphere (your job, your hobby) is none of your spouse's business
- The excuse that you are not good at talking (you need to learn!)
- The spoken or unspoken demand that your spouse tell you everything and listen to everything (a barrage of questions or chatter discourages quiet people)
- Reluctance to "burden" your spouse
- Fear of rejection or contempt
- Harsh ways of speaking (accusation, loudness, impatience, speculating about the other's motives)

Make Christ central. Unless your marriage is built on the rock of Christ, the storms of life (illness, loss of job, aging, busy schedules, a money squeeze) can easily smash it (Luke 6:47-49). Going to church is not enough; you should pray together daily about issues you are facing. Search the Scriptures together when you have a decision to make. Learning to tell your spouse your prayer needs and expressing your true feelings to God with him or her present is a great boost to communication between you. Prayer together seems scary or hard to schedule at first, but it is crucial.

WHAT DOES SUBMISSION MEAN?

God established an authority structure in families "to focus and safeguard a couple's unity. Avoiding both the false unity of domination and the disunity of anarchy, he offers us the way that he himself takes—headship and submission in the Spirit of love." As the Son is in total submission to His loving Father, so the wife is to her husband. "The wife's submission does not mean that she is passive, inferior, unequal, or immature, nor does the husband's authority say that he is better, smarter, or more important. There is an equality of worth between husband and wife, yet a distinction of responsibilities."[1]

The balance between authority and submission enables the couple to get the job done because "It does away with the struggle for power that paralyzes many marriages. It enables a couple to settle minor decisions quickly, saving their discussion for more important matters."[2]

When decisions affecting the life of the whole family must be made, husband and wife should discuss the matter together thoroughly, looking for God's direction. Ordinarily, couples who discuss these decisions can reach an agreement on them. If they cannot, it is the husband's responsibility to decide how to settle the issue. He might exercise his authority by deciding to wait until the two of them can reach an agreement. He might decide to follow his wife's opinion, or to follow his own, or to seek outside counsel. The fact of his headship does not mean that the husband makes all the decisions by himself, or even that, in a conflict, his opinions must prevail. He seeks always to do what is wise and what is right.[3]

Submission includes obeying decisions you disagree with, but *not* those that violate God's law or your conscience. That is, it does not include putting up with violence or adultery. In areas to which the Bible does not speak explicitly but on which you have convictions (see pages 155–158), don't violate your conscience, but do examine it. Make sure that your convictions are biblically based and that you are not using "convictions" as an excuse to insist on your own way.

Submission works best in a family when you are part of a larger Christian community. If the husband is experiencing what it feels like to submit to authority over him, he will be more gentle in the way he exercises his own authority. If you are part of a severely authoritarian community, consider switching to a more balanced fellowship (see pages 137–140).

WHAT ARE THE BIGGEST THREATS TO A MARRIAGE?

In *Love for a Lifetime*, James Dobson lists these potentially disastrous problems:

- Overcommitment and physical exhaustion
- Excessive debt and conflict over how money will be spent
- Selfishness
- Interference from in-laws
- Unrealistic expectations
- Suffocating the spouse with jealousy, domination, and so on
- Alcohol or substance abuse
- Pornography, gambling, and other addictions
- Sexual frustration, loneliness, low self-esteem, and the greener grass of infidelity
- Business failure
- Business success
- Getting married too young[4]

Avoid or repent of these harmful conditions in yourself. Talk with your spouse about those that involve both of you. If you think your spouse is guilty of one, see the answer to the next question.

WHAT IF MY MARRIAGE IS TERRIBLY PAINFUL?

Ideally, you and your spouse should be best friends and perfect complements for each other. But because of sin, there will be clashes. If your spouse doesn't seem to care about loving or respecting you, don't despair:

God totally loves and values you, so your survival and joy do not depend on your spouse's responses. Rich fellowship with God can fill up your empty place.

God is all-powerful, all-wise, and all-loving, so you can trust that He is using your painful situation for your good and His glory. He will use the areas in which you and your spouse rub against each other to smooth down your sharp edges and teach you humility, patience, forgiveness, and selflessness. Suffering gives you a chance to glorify God before all the angels by your loving, trusting, nonbitter response.

Use the steps of forgiveness often (see page 174).

Other believers can help bear your burden of rejection and enable you to feel God's love and respect. Find a small group of intimate friends with whom you can share Christ's love (see "Starting a Small Group" on page 141).

WHAT ABOUT DIVORCE?

God's intent is to join a man and a woman permanently (Matthew 19:3-6).

God permitted divorce "because your hearts were hard" (Matthew 19:8). Sinful people are incapable of keeping a commitment to love, so God allowed divorce among the Jews.

For the same reason:

If your non-Christian spouse asks for a divorce and there seems to be no hope of reconciliation, let your spouse go. Paul says that this is the way to uphold peace. You are not in adultery if you remarry in that case (1 Corinthians 7:12-16).

Believers should not initiate divorce except for unfaithfulness.

> Anyone who divorces his wife, except for marital unfaithfulness, and marries another woman commits adultery. (Matthew 19:9)

Some Christians interpret this to forbid remarriage except if the marriage covenant has been broken through unchastity. Others feel that God allows divorce and remarriage in the case of a wider understanding of unfaithfulness:

- Desertion
- Physical or verbal cruelty
- Denial of conjugal rights
- Substance abuse (alcoholism, drug abuse)

In any case, a Christian should never go into marriage with the idea that divorce is an option if it doesn't work out. Biblically based teachers

all regard divorce as something like cutting up a living body, as a kind of surgical operation. Some of them think the operation so violent that it cannot be done at all; others admit it as a desperate remedy in extreme cases. They are all agreed that it is more like having both your legs cut off than it is like dissolving a business partnership or even deserting a regiment. What they all disagree with is the modern view that it is a simple readjustment of partners, to be made whenever people feel they are no longer in love with one another, or when either of them falls in love with someone else.[5]

REARING CHILDREN

Train a child in the way he should go, and when he is old he will not turn from it.

PROVERBS 22:6

WHAT IS THE BIBLICAL GOAL OF REARING CHILDREN?

The apostle Paul instructs, "Fathers, do not exasperate your children; instead, bring them up in the training and instruction of the Lord" (Ephesians 6:4).

The parents' goal is to raise children who know and love the Lord and who follow His ways. Fathers bear the primary responsibility for this, but mothers share it. More specifically, parents should train their children to:

- Pray
- Worship
- Read the Bible with understanding and benefit
- Turn to Jesus when in need
- Know the central truths of the faith
- Love others
- Love self
- Obey authority

- Control their impulses
- Act responsibly
- Deal with the moral conflicts of secular life
- Manage the skills of living on earth (toothbrushing, mathematics, driving a car, and so on)

Loving others includes respecting parents and other authorities, serving others selflessly, speaking correctly to siblings (without fighting or putting each other down), repenting for wrongdoing, and practicing forgiveness. Parents shouldn't expect two-year-olds to learn selflessness (it's developmentally impossible), nor should they expect more perfection in any area from teenagers than the parents themselves have learned. But teaching children to love the Lord and follow His ways should be goals of training.

HOW CAN I TRAIN MY CHILDREN AND MEET BIBLICAL GOALS?

Give a lot of affection. The surest way to raise a hard-hearted person, who mistrusts the Father God and can't open himself to others, is to deny him affection as a child. Children need lots of holding, hugging, playing, laughing, and talking with their parents. This is especially important for fathers, who are less likely to have daily contact with each child. Many counselors believe that children gain security in their identities as men or women from clean affection from fathers.

Children need eye contact when you talk, scheduled time alone with you (without the other kids), and attentive listening. They need to learn to trust you, to be secure that they are loved and valued. Otherwise, your discipline will seem cruel and your teaching will bounce off a wounded, calloused heart.

Lead by example. Affection is one example you need to set. Your children want to be just like you, and in many ways they will be. Knowing this will enable you to act as a good example for them. In addition, your children need to see you:

- Say "please" and "thank you"
- Pray
- Read and discuss the Bible
- Talk to your spouse considerately
- Speak positively about coworkers
- Handle family crises with grace and trust
- Rejoice in your Christian life, even in hardships
- Work for a living

Use verbal teaching. Children can't learn to pray just by watching you kneel in silence. You have to explain what you are doing. Likewise, you might want to show them where the Bible says not to fight or complain (this sets an example; we get our standards from the Bible), explain why this is important, and remind them continually that this is a family expectation. The Israelites were commanded to "impress" God's words onto their children's hearts through constant repetition (Deuteronomy 6:7-9) and to explain God's saving acts that lay behind the rules (6:20-21).

Teaching should go on throughout life's daily events. Encourage your children to ask why and to tell you how they feel about what happens to them. Be available to talk. Set aside the time at the dinner table to discuss attitudes and values about an issue. Bedtime may be good for hearing about and dealing with feelings about the day's events. Consider taking time for each child alone each week to talk and play. Good questions to ask are, "Did anything make you sad (happy, mad, and so on) today (this week)?"[1] Once you've thoroughly heard the child's story, explain gently how Christians respond to rejection or anger. Show that you care with hugs, eye contact, and your tone of voice. Notice that *listening* to a child is crucial for spontaneous teaching.

Planned, systematic, and repeated teaching of complex chores and behaviors is as necessary as informal teaching. It is unfair to expect a child to wash or paint a wall without thorough example and explanation. Children don't know that too much sugar is harmful unless they are told why in simple terms.

Practice consistent discipline. Discipline teaches a child the consequences of disobedience. Children need to feel something unpleasant after a wrong action to really grasp that it is wrong. Later this will help them understand why God judges sin. Children also need to know that parents are strong enough to deserve their respect and trust so that their world is secure. Children usually prefer to resolve guilt through swift, fair punishment.

> Folly is bound up in the heart of a child,
>> but the rod of discipline will drive it far from him. (Proverbs 22:15)

> A servant cannot be corrected by mere words;
>> though he understands, he will not respond. (Proverbs 29:19)

Reason alone does not work because, like adults, children are naturally rebellious, self-centered sinners.

God expresses His love for us partly by disciplining us to move us to the peace of a righteous life (Hebrews 12:5-11; Proverbs 13:24). Sparing children the pain of discipline dooms them to a life of conflict, confusion, and misery. Your children won't be harmed by your discipline if you follow these guidelines:

- Show them lots of affection when not disciplining them.
- Deal with your angers and frustrations so that you aren't tempted to take them out on a disobedient child.
- Be consistent.
- Make the rules clear.
- Punish quickly after the crime is discovered.
- Punish in private (even a child's dignity is fragile).
- Never humiliate with names, ridicule, or a punishment that they clearly find demeaning.

Consistency means the same punishment follows the same crime always; your mood doesn't make you more harsh or more lenient. Inconsistency teaches children not to avoid wrong behavior but to avoid you when you are in a bad mood. Consistency also means parental unity.

Don't punish a child if you haven't ever explained that the action is wrong—and why. Don't punish if your actual words gave the child a choice ("Wouldn't you like to . . . ?").

Small children can remember only so many rules. Select those that are crucial for their safety and a tolerable home environment, and enforce them consistently. Then, train the children to obey you when you give a specific instruction. Toddler-proofing a house is generally easier than rebuking children every time they touch something they should not.

Let the punishment fit the crime. Only a few misdeeds (willfully disobeying parents, damaging property on purpose) deserve your ultimate punishment. (Some experts advocate a solid but controlled spanking, while others are opposed to spanking.) In other cases, consequences should relate rationally to the misdeed (this is how the real world works). For instance, if after a repeated verbal training and example, a child doesn't say "please," explain that he won't get what he asks for unless he says "please." Or something that has been misused could be taken away for a time.

Logical consequences are especially important for older children, whereas very young children respond best to a simple, controlled, physical signal. Sometimes, instead of or in addition to punishment, a child really needs to sleep or to discuss some frustration that is bothering him.

Involve your children in your goals. Children learn to be responsible as you let them become gradually more involved in the decisions that affect them. Well before teen age, start involving your children in setting the punishment that will go with each rule. Give them an allowance (and if possible, ways to earn extra money) and a savings account, and teach them to save for what they want. Of course, even though you involve them in these decisions, you always remain the ultimate authority as long as they live under your roof.

Be a united front. In order to avoid confusing children with contradictory signals, parents need to agree on what they want to teach. They need to set consistent examples and agree on the discipline that will go with each kind of infraction. The father must stand behind the mother's decision and action, and vice versa. Children learn to play one parent against the other when there is disunity.

Seek support from other Christians. Seek emotional and prayer support from other believers. Talk about what works and what doesn't. Be refreshed by group Bible study, prayer, and teaching. Show your children by example how you talk, share, and worship with others.

Remember the long-range view. You will see rebellion along the way, but God promises ultimate victory if you are patient. Remember that you are training your children in the way *they* should go. That is, you want them to reflect the Lord's character in their particular personalities and vocations. Don't assume that God wants your children to be in full-time professional "ministry" or to have the career you think is the most respectable.

HOW CAN I TRAIN MY CHILDREN IN THE BIBLE AND PRAYER WITHOUT BORING THEM?[2]

Be consistent. Choose a time that you can maintain day after day, such as first thing in the morning, before or after dinner, or at bedtime. Don't allow children to schedule activities that interfere with that time of praying and learning from the Bible together. Teenagers require more freedom to choose their activities, but you should be able to schedule some time with them at least once or twice a week.

Be sensitive to age level.

Toddlers can focus on a lesson for only three or four minutes. They need a short bit of teaching, a song, and a brief prayer. They learn by *repetition*—the same song or truth sung or recited or restated many times a day for several days. Some toddlers prefer to watch, but most like to *get involved*. They like to use all of their senses—taste, touch, and smell as well as sight. Puppets, pictures, flannel boards, crayons, songs, games, and the chance to sit on a parent's lap to hear a story will make most toddlers eager for "devotions."

Toddlers learn when they watch, do, then do again and again. Because daily repetition is essential in teaching them, Sunday school can't possibly do the job alone.

Toddlers will accept unquestioningly anything they are told by someone they trust, so this is the ideal age to begin spiritual training. They can learn:

- A concept of God—who He is, His character, His attributes
- Love and respect for the Bible
- How to pray
- Kindness toward others
- Obedience to God and parents
- Common Bible characters

Elementary-age children are learning to relate, think for themselves, define and act on moral values, and deal with feelings. They like involvement, action, and learning. They can increasingly grasp concepts like:

- Salvation
- Identifying publicly with Christ
- Honesty versus cheating and lying
- Obedience
- Loyalty
- Friendship

Preteens like identifying with a group, so your devotional time can be a chance to let them enjoy belonging to your family. They like structure, consistency, telling and acting out stories, competition, and a lot of physical activity. Plays, Scripture memory contests, visual aids, walks in the woods, Bible games, and role playing are ideal. Interest them in prayer by putting them in charge of keeping a family prayer record book with requests in one column and answers in the other.

Fifteen or twenty minutes should be the maximum time you expect a preteen to attend to prayer and Bible learning. However, if you gear the topic to something of immediate concern to the child (broken friendships, doubting God's love, family conflicts), you may get longer and more enthusiastic involvement.

Emphasize *memorizing* and *meditating* on Scripture verses. Read them, recite them, visualize facts through pictures and games, internalize truths through discussion, apply truths by taking your children on service projects and practicing godly living at home and school.

Teach an *overview of the Bible,* the basics of what's in each Testament.

Emphasize *prayer*. Encourage children to tell God just how

they feel and what they want. Teach them why some requests are answered "yes," some "no," and some "wait." Use songs, psalms, and your own example to teach praise and thanksgiving. Model confession, and have children practice it whenever they do wrong.

Teenagers need to learn to think and choose independently of their parents. They question everything, especially the values and truths they learned from their parents. They rebel when parents try to force them to continue to obey unquestioningly. The big issue they are struggling with is identity—who am I, what do I believe, and what do I want to do with myself? They need parents who will stay alongside to discuss and add counsel but rarely give orders. They should be free to negotiate the times and contents of devotions, to be silent during prayer and discussions, and sometimes even to be absent. They crave respect. Serious discussion of biblical passages should replace puppets and games. Concentrate on the passages that deal with identity and values (who Jesus is, resisting temptation, convictions about success and relationships), and be open to having your views challenged. You can make your disagreement clear while showing that you respect your children for thinking for themselves, and that you love them no matter what they say. Teach them that some truths are accepted by faith, but that they certainly shouldn't abandon intelligent reasoning.

Provide variety. This is the key to holding children's interest. Pray with psalms one day, then the next day let each person pray one sentence in turn. Use puppets to show a story about Jesus, then act out an Old Testament story, then spend a day or two learning verses from the Bible. Practice memory verses briefly each day, then plan one day for a memory contest. You don't have to do something creative every day, just often enough to maintain pleasurable anticipation. Planning shouldn't take more than twenty minutes a week once you've had some practice.

MANAGING MONEY[1]

People who long to be rich fall into temptation and are trapped by many foolish and harmful desires that plunge them into ruin and destruction.

1 TIMOTHY 6:9, NLT

ARE MONEY AND POSSESSIONS GOOD, EVIL, OR MORALLY NEUTRAL?

God created the material world, and He declared it "very good" (Genesis 1:31). Material things such as food, clothing, and land are not evil, nor even morally neutral, but good.

God created money. Throughout history, money has been a simple way to store value. If we didn't have money, we would have to carry valuables such as livestock and grain from the farm and trade them directly for other goods. God allowed Israel to use gold and silver to represent material goods as a *medium of exchange*, a *store of value*, and a *standard of value* (Deuteronomy 14:24-27). Because the goods themselves are created good, the money that represents them is good.

God created capital. Capital is any asset that produces continuing benefits. Human capital is physical and mental abilities, which can be enhanced by training, education, and experience. Material capital consists of land, livestock, buildings, factories, equipment, businesses, and so on. Money is the third form of capital. It is unique in that it is productive only when converted into one of the other forms of capital. Because God created capital, it is good. Every economic system in the world uses capital.

God created income. Income is the increase produced by capital. When He established His model society in Israel, God gave each extended family a piece of land (material capital) to be worked with labor (human capital) to produce crops (income). God did not intend for the land capital to be consumed, so He taught Israel in great detail how to use both income and capital. Income, then, is also good, provided that it is used according to God's priorities.

WHO OWNS THE THINGS I POSSESS?
God owns everything in the world.

> The land is mine and you are but aliens and my tenants. Throughout the country that you hold as a possession, you must provide for the redemption of the land. (Leviticus 25:23-24)

> "The silver is mine and the gold is mine," declares the LORD Almighty. (Haggai 2:8)

God made us His stewards. God made us in His image and appointed us to exercise dominion over His creation as His stewards for His purposes (Genesis 1:26). A "steward" is a manager. Jesus told several parables that portray God as a landowner and humans as the servants He has placed in charge of His possessions in His absence (Matthew 25:14-30; Luke 16:1-13; 19:12-27).

This is the New Testament's basic teaching on stewardship: *We must use what God has entrusted to us productively and faithfully.* This means that we must invest our resources to produce an increase that contributes to God's aims (Luke 16:10-11; 19:12-13; 1 Corinthians 4:2).

For the most part, individuals own the possessions God has entrusted to them. Being in God's image means in part that we have diverse personalities and individual responsibility and freedom to make moral choices. God entrusts responsibility for material possessions primarily to individuals. As far as God is concerned, we are stewards under His ownership. But in the Bible, individuals are generally described as owning what they have.

FOR WHAT PURPOSES HAS GOD ENTRUSTED POSSESSIONS TO ME?
Enjoying His material blessings.

God . . . richly provides us with everything for our enjoyment.
(1 Timothy 6:17)

Paul warned the Colossian Christians not to let people impose rules about what they could eat, drink, and do (Colossians 2:16-23).

Such regulations indeed have an appearance of wisdom, with their self-imposed worship, their false humility and their harsh treatment of the body, but they lack any value in restraining sensual indulgence. (Colossians 2:23)

Because God's material creation is good, we should not feel guilty about enjoying it, provided that we avoid the seductions of materialism, covetousness, and possessiveness.

Using our individual possessions to build up community. While there is a sense in which we are individuals, unique and personally responsible for our moral choices, we are also corporate, made to live in community. We are responsible for others' needs, not just our own. Our model is Christ, who selflessly gave up what was rightfully His for others (Philippians 2:4-7). The financial priorities in both the Old and New Testaments are as follows:

Providing for family.

But if a widow has children or grandchildren, these should learn first of all to put their religion into practice by caring for their own family and so repaying their parents and grandparents, for this is pleasing to God. . . . If anyone does not provide for his relatives, and especially for his immediate family, he has denied the faith and is worse than an unbeliever. (1 Timothy 5:4,8)

Under this category of caring for needs should come basic family necessities, such as food, clothing, housing, education, medical care, and providing for future emergencies. Comforts beyond necessities are good, not evil, but they should be lower in priority than the following list of responsibilities.

Providing for Christian brothers and sisters in difficulty.

> If anyone has material possessions and sees his brother in
> need but has no pity on him, how can the love of God be in
> him? . . . Let us not love with words or tongue but with actions
> and in truth. (1 John 3:17-18)

The Bible emphasizes personal giving from one believer to another (Romans 12:13). Other believers' interests are equal to and even greater than our own (Philippians 2:1-8). When we see a need, we should respond, and we must be alert to see needs.

Providing for the poor, for widows, and for the children who lack one or both parents.

> If a man shuts his ears to the cry of the poor,
>
> > he too will cry out and not be answered. (Proverbs 21:13)

John the Baptist advised "fruit in keeping with repentance" (Luke 3:8):

> The man with two tunics should share with him who has none,
> and the one who has food should do the same. (Luke 3:11)

Jesus and His disciples gave to the poor (John 12:5), and people in Acts are praised for giving to the poor (Acts 9:36; 10:2,31).

In the Old Testament, widows and orphans are singled out (Deuteronomy 10:18; 14:25-29) because they were especially vulnerable in ancient society. Single parents and their children are somewhat more secure today, but they often have financial and other needs.

The federal welfare system makes it easy for us in the United States to feel that if we pay our taxes, we are released from responsibility to the poor. However, we are still responsible as Christian individuals and groups to help the poor. In general, the best way to help a poor person is to provide capital in the form of training, education, a job, or material needed to work productively (as well as the personal encouragement that builds hope). For some Old Testament approaches to helping the poor, see Leviticus 19:9-10; 25:1-55; Deuteronomy 23:19-20,24-25; 24:6,10-15,17-21.

Providing for spiritual leaders.

Anyone who receives instruction in the word must share all good things with his instructor. (Galatians 6:6)

The New Testament commands us to support those who minister to us, whether pastors and elders in our home churches or traveling teachers and leaders (Luke 8:1-3; 9:1-5; 10:1-7; 1 Corinthians 9:11-18; 1 Timothy 5:17-18; Titus 3:13-14; 3 John 6-8).

Giving to the church. Beyond supporting our local spiritual leaders, we also have to pay for whatever buildings and programs we think are necessary for worship, teaching, and Christian community. The early church had minimal expenses because believers met in homes, but if we want more elaborate buildings and programs, we have to pay for them.

Showing hospitality to travelers and strangers.

> Do not forget to entertain strangers, for by so doing some people
> have entertained angels without knowing it. (Hebrews 13:2)

The idea here is not social entertaining (which is okay but is done for pleasure or business reasons) but the kind of selfless love that goes out of its way for those in need. Missionaries, traveling teachers, and other Christians passing through town are singled out for mention in the New Testament.

> Dear friend, you are faithful in what you are doing for the broth-
> ers, even though they are strangers to you. They have told the
> church about your love. You will do well to send them on their
> way in a manner worthy of God. It was for the sake of the
> Name that they went out. (3 John 5-7)

Giving for the extension of the gospel. This item is last in this list but not last in priority. In fact, it permeates all of the preceding items. Providing for one's family, fellow Christians, and other poor people is a practical testimony that we have Christ's attitude of selfless concern for others. It "make[s] the teaching about God our Savior attractive" (Titus 2:10) and so serves the extension of the gospel. Providing for churches, local spiritual leaders, and traveling missionaries and teachers also serves this end. But we should make it a priority to support missionaries not only when they travel through our town, but also when they are in the field.

Paul spoke of the Philippians who supported his ministry not as "donors" but as *partners* in the gospel with him (Philippians 1:5).

He had a personal, loving relationship with them that undergirded and motivated their financial support.

WHAT SHOULD BE MY ATTITUDES ABOUT GIVING?

Giving is a blessing to giver and receiver. Paul speaks of "the privilege of sharing in this service to the saints" (2 Corinthians 8:4). Even in their "extreme poverty" (8:2), the Christians of Macedonia found giving to be such a privilege that they insisted that Paul let them do it.

Giving allows us to reflect God's character. God is a giver by nature (John 3:16; Romans 8:32; Philippians 2:5-8), and Christians naturally desire to be like Him.

Giving builds community and brotherhood. When we act as partners sharing finances generously and humbly, love is strengthened.

> Their hearts will go out to you, because of the surpassing grace
> God has given you. Thanks be to God for his indescribable gift!
> (2 Corinthians 9:14-15)

Here, the "indescribable gift" is partly the bond of love among all the givers and also between them and the receivers.

Giving produces maturity.

> We want you to know about the grace that God has given the
> Macedonian churches. . . . See that you also excel in this grace
> of giving. (2 Corinthians 8:1,7; see also 9:10)

Giving allows God to give to the giver. The New Testament emphasizes the spiritual rewards of giving, although material rewards are also possible.

> Do not store up for yourselves treasures on earth, where moth and rust destroy, and where thieves break in and steal. But store up for yourselves treasures in heaven, where moth and rust do not destroy, and where thieves do not break in and steal. For where your treasure is, there your heart will be also. (Matthew 6:19-21)

> Give, and it will be given to you. A good measure, pressed down, shaken together and running over, will be poured into your lap. For with the measure you use, it will be measured to you. (Luke 6:38)

To the Philippians, who gave to his ministry with no thought for repayment, Paul wrote, "My God will meet all your needs according to his glorious riches in Christ Jesus" (Philippians 4:19). Because Paul and the Philippians were partners in ministry, they shared the spiritual rewards that Paul was storing up in heaven (Philippians 4:17). Likewise, if we act as ministry partners, we share in the spiritual rewards.

Philippians 4:19 is not a promise that God will supply all our material wants. For one thing, it speaks of *needs*, not desires. Further, Paul addresses these words to people who are giving selflessly, out of love, not out of a desire for a material reward. Jesus tells us to give "without expecting to get anything back" (Luke 6:35).

In the Old Testament, God made many promises to bless Israel materially as a result of generous giving. Christians are divided as to whether those promises apply to Christians, or whether the blessings of giving are now mainly spiritual. The important thing is that God looks at the heart. If we give for an earthly reward, then we forfeit our heavenly reward (Matthew 6:2).

Giving produces many positive results.

Giving causes thanksgiving and praise.

Through us your generosity will result in thanksgiving to God. This service that you perform is not only supplying the needs of God's people but is also overflowing in many expressions of thanks to God. Because of the service by which you have proved yourselves, men will praise God for the obedience that accompanies your confession of the gospel of Christ, and for your generosity in sharing with them and with everyone else. (2 Corinthians 9:11-13)

Giving causes rejoicing.

I rejoice greatly in the Lord that at last you have renewed your concern for me. (Philippians 4:10)

Giving causes prayer.

I always pray with joy because of your partnership in the gospel from the first day until now. (Philippians 1:4-5)

Giving encourages others to give.

I know your eagerness to help, and I have been boasting about it to the Macedonians, telling them that since last year you in Achaia were ready to give; and your enthusiasm has stirred most of them to action. (2 Corinthians 9:2)

"It is more blessed to give than to receive" (Acts 20:35). Therefore, we should order our finances so that we will be in a position to give as much as possible, not so that we will constantly be on the receiving end of others' generosity. We should not be ashamed or too proud to receive, but our goal should be to give more often than we receive.

Some people feel that working at a lucrative profession and saving for the future reflect an unwillingness to depend on God for daily needs. However, the Bible praises, never rebukes, honest earning, planning, and saving.

Giving must be voluntary. Certain Old Testament financial requirements were mandatory (Exodus 13:1-16; 23:19; Leviticus 27:3-32). To withhold from God a tenth of one's income, the first-fruits of the harvest, and the price of every firstborn animal and person was to "rob God" (Malachi 3:8-10). Many Christians feel that 10 percent is the minimum amount we owe God and His work (the firstfruit laws are rarely applied literally). However, in their extensive teaching on giving, neither Jesus nor Paul makes the tithe a law. Instead, they emphasize voluntary giving as an expression of love.

> I am not commanding you [to give a certain amount], but I want to test the sincerity of your love by comparing it with the earnestness of others. For you know the grace of our Lord Jesus Christ, that though he was rich, yet for your sakes he became poor, so that you through his poverty might become rich. (2 Corinthians 8:8-9)

On the other hand, many Christians who do not regard the tithe as a law believe that if one is unwilling to give even 10 percent, one has not grasped the principles of generosity, contentment, and the blessing of giving.

As you decide how much of your income to set aside, ask the Lord to cleanse your heart from rationalizations and excuses. Ten percent is a good starting point for disciplining yourself.

Giving must be cheerful.

> Do not be hardhearted or tightfisted toward your poor brother. Rather be openhanded and freely lend him whatever he needs. Be careful not to harbor this wicked thought: "The seventh year, the year for canceling debts, is near." . . . Give generously to him and do so without a grudging heart. (Deuteronomy 15:7-10)

> Each man should give what he has decided in his heart to give, not reluctantly or under compulsion, for God loves a cheerful giver. (2 Corinthians 9:7)

We give not because God will punish us if we don't but

because we love God and people and are grateful to God for the bounty He has provided.

Also, we must never judge others for giving less than we think they could.

> Who are you to judge someone else's servant? To his own master he stands or falls. And he will stand, for the Lord is able to make him stand. . . . Each one should be fully convinced in his own mind. . . . You, then, why do you judge your brother? Or why do you look down on your brother? (Romans 14:4-5,10)

The amount of our giving is to be proportionate to our income. Ten percent is a good place to start. But affluent Christians—when they escape the traps of materialism and covetousness—generally find they can increase the proportion of their income spent on others' needs.

Those who are not affluent should understand that they are still responsible to give and that their giving makes a difference (Luke 21:1-4; 2 Corinthians 8:11-12). God is interested in the attitudes of the heart, not in the size of the gift.

Giving must be generous.

> Remember this: Whoever sows sparingly will also reap sparingly, and whoever sows generously will also reap generously. (2 Corinthians 9:6)

God is generous and takes every opportunity to express His generosity. He is pleased when we reflect His character.

Giving should be regular and systematic. Paul suggested that the Corinthians set aside their gifts each week (1 Corinthians 16:2). He was aware of the discrepancies that develop between our intentions and our actions, so he suggested a weekly discipline. Although there is nothing universal about the weekly arrangement, it is necessary to plan our giving.

Giving should be without display.

Be careful not to do your "acts of righteousness" before men, to be seen by them. If you do, you will have no reward from your Father in heaven.

So when you give to the needy, do not announce it with trumpets, as the hypocrites do in the synagogues and on the streets, to be honored by men. I tell you the truth, they have received their reward in full. But when you give to the needy, do not let your left hand know what your right hand is doing, so that your giving may be in secret. (Matthew 6:1-4)

Again, the important thing in God's eyes is the motivation, not the action.

HOW CAN I AFFORD TO GIVE MY MONEY?

The key is not the magnitude of your income but your attitudes:

The kingdom of God comes first. When Jesus called His disciples, many of them had to drop their professions to follow Him (Matthew 4:18-19; Mark 2:14). In return for their commitment, He promised no material reward, not even a place to sleep (Matthew 8:20). Love for Jesus had to come before family love and even love for one's own life (Matthew 10:37-39; Luke 14:26-33). In return, Jesus' disciples would receive treasures in heaven, true life, and provision for this life (Matthew 6:25-34).

> And everyone who has left houses or brothers or sisters or father or mother or children or fields for my sake will receive a hundred times as much [not necessarily materially] and will inherit eternal life. (Matthew 19:29)

The material things of which Jesus spoke in Matthew 6 are not wrong, for they are God's provision. But if given priority as the objects of life, they become idols, and so they must be kept in perspective.

Faith should replace worry.

> Do not worry about your life, what you will eat or drink; or about your body, what you will wear. Is not life more important than food, and the body more important than clothes? Look at the birds of the air; they do not sow or reap or store away in barns, and yet your heavenly Father feeds them. Are you not much more valuable than they? Who of you by worrying can add a single hour to his life?
>
> And why do you worry about clothes? See how the lilies of the field grow. They do not labor or spin. Yet I tell you that not even Solomon in all his splendor was dressed like one of these. If that is how God clothes the grass of the field, which is here today and tomorrow is thrown into the fire, will he not much more clothe you, O you of little faith? So do not worry, saying,

"What shall we eat?" or "What shall we drink?" or "What shall we wear?" For the pagans run after all these things, and your heavenly Father knows that you need them. But seek first his kingdom and his righteousness, and all these things will be given to you as well. Therefore do not worry about tomorrow, for tomorrow will worry about itself. Each day has enough trouble of its own. (Matthew 6:25-34)

The essence of Jesus' message about material things is simply "Do not worry" because God provides adequately. Underlying this exhortation are more important issues: the allegiance of our hearts, the attitudes of our minds, our reason for existence, and the source of our confidence. If we are seeking God's kingdom first, if we are giving generously, if we are prayerfully and thankfully depending on God, if we are avoiding covetousness and materialism, then we can confidently rely on God to meet our needs.

Jesus' words about faith and dependence on God do not negate the other biblical admonitions to be diligent, frugal, hardworking, good stewards, and careful planners. We are actively trusting God to enable us to fulfill the responsibilities listed earlier in the topic "For what purposes has God entrusted possessions to me?"

We should have dominion over material things, not be slaves to them.

No one can serve two masters. Either he will hate the one and love the other, or he will be devoted to the one and despise the other. You cannot serve both God and Money. (Matthew 6:24)

Materialism is making money and material possessions the goal of life—our god. Jesus warns repeatedly against the dangers of materialism (Luke 12:15; 15:13; 16:15). What are the signs of materialism, and how can they be avoided?

Possessiveness.

The ground of a certain rich man produced a good crop. He thought to himself, "What shall I do? I have no place to store my crops."

Then he said, "This is what I'll do. I will tear down my barns and build bigger ones, and there I will store all my grain and my goods. And I'll say to myself, 'You have plenty of good things laid up for many years. Take life easy; eat, drink and be merry.'"

But God said to him, "You fool! This very night your life will be demanded from you. Then who will get what you have prepared for yourself?"

This is how it will be with anyone who stores up things for himself but is not rich toward God. (Luke 12:16-21)

Hoarding possessions is "meaningless—a miserable business!" (Ecclesiastes 4:8). If you are tempted to accumulate more than you need for your family's requirements (including saving for emergencies, retirement, and so on), ask yourself what your goal is. Are you making wise eternal investments, or hoarding what you will never use?

The opposite of possessiveness is generosity, which proves far wiser in the long run. (See pages 224–230.)

Preoccupation with material things.

> For the love of money is a root of all kinds of evil. Some people, eager for money, have wandered from the faith and pierced themselves with many griefs. (1 Timothy 6:10)

If you find yourself thinking and worrying about finances, ask God to free you from preoccupation with material things and help you trust Him.

Covetousness.

> You shall not covet. . . . You shall not set your desire on . . . anything that belongs to your neighbor. (Deuteronomy 5:21)

While possessiveness is clinging to one's own possessions, covetousness is craving someone else's. Covetousness is idolatry (Ephesians 5:5; Colossians 3:5). It is the love of things rather than God or people. Signs of covetousness are the desire to gain wealth quickly and the inability to be satisfied with what one has. The more one has, the more one wants (Ecclesiastes 5:10; James 4:1-3).

The opposite of covetousness is contentment. Contentment means that we are willing to accept ourselves as God created us, with our gifts, talents, and opportunities. Contentment in regard to material things is an active, not passive, acceptance. Being content enables us to accept the responsibility that accompanies our calling and situation.

Paul accepted his situation in life even though it involved hardship and a variety of financial circumstances:

I have learned to be content whatever the circumstances. I know what it is to be in need, and I know what it is to have plenty. I have learned the secret of being content in any and every situation, whether well fed or hungry, whether living in plenty or in want. (Philippians 4:11-12)

Contentment is not easy when we are surrounded by people to whom we tend to compare ourselves and whose respect we desire. The solution is to saturate our minds with God's Word so that we recognize the negative results of covetousness and possessiveness.

Our confidence must be in God, not self, as the source of goods.

You may say to yourself, "My power and the strength of my hands have produced this wealth for me." But remember the LORD your God, for it is he who gives you the ability to produce wealth, and so confirms his covenant, which he swore to your forefathers, as it is today. (Deuteronomy 8:17-18)

One reason why people worry and become possessive and covetous is they think that survival depends on themselves and that material success is a reason for pride. But survival depends on God, honest material success is a reason for humble gratitude, and dishonest success is a reason for shame and a promise of disaster.

Our confidence must be in God, not wealth, as the source of security. Wealth is unreliable. We can't take it with us into eternity (Luke 12:16-21). But further, we can't even guarantee that it won't vanish suddenly in this life (Proverbs 23:4-5). And thirdly, even if we hold on to it, wealth cannot bring satisfaction (Ecclesiastes 5:10).

Be honest.

> Dishonest money dwindles away,
>> but he who gathers money little by little makes it grow.
>>> (Proverbs 13:11)

Wealth gained dishonestly or by hurting others tends to disappear quickly. But even if a person grows on dishonest wealth, his life is twisted, shriveled, and ultimately empty.

> Better a little with the fear of the LORD
>> than great wealth with turmoil. (Proverbs 15:16)

God stresses honesty in His Laws for Israel.

> For the LORD your God detests anyone who does these things, anyone who deals dishonestly. (Deuteronomy 25:16)

Is wealth worth having God detest you?

Live below your income.

> The wise man saves for the future, but the foolish man spends whatever he gets. (Proverbs 21:20, TLB)

Now we come to the practical steps. If you spend everything you earn, you have no margin for error or emergency. Debt is inevitable. But if you resist materialism and grow contentment, living below your income is almost always possible.

Establish priorities. If you live below your income, then you have at least a small surplus to begin planning your priorities. The details are up to you, but here is a suggested sequence:

Basic essentials:

- Taxes and debts (automatic responsibilities)
- Basic giving (putting God first)
- Basic family needs (food, housing, education, medical)
- Saving for a margin (insurance a partial option)

Surplus. Beyond the essentials are two surplus tracks, both of which must be *pursued simultaneously*. Establishing priorities and a balance between the two tracks is at the discretion of the individual or family, with guidance from God.

Increased Giving   Secondary Family Needs (clothing, transportation, recreation)

Increased Giving   Saving for Capital

Increased Giving   Family Amenities (convenience and comfort)

Increased Giving   Personal Amenities (travel, luxuries, and so on)[2]

Master your credit card. Buying on credit is living beyond your income, using tomorrow's income to purchase what you want today. It may reflect materialism, covetousness, impatience, and lack of self-control. It is also expensive, because interest adds dramatically to the cost of things.

> The rich rule over the poor,
>> and the borrower is servant to the lender. (Proverbs 22:7)

The Bible does not forbid buying on credit, but it warns against it. Most Christian financial counselors advise people to use credit only for items that rise in value, such as houses and businesses. Items that drop in value, such as refrigerators, cars, and so on, should be bought with cash.

For those who can resist the temptation to overspend and pay off their bill in full when they receive it, many Christian counselors accept the use of charge cards. We will be much less likely to have financial problems if we:

- Honor God with our finances and trust Him to meet our needs (Philippians 4:19)
- Learn contentment (Philippians 4:11-12)
- Learn patience and self-control (Galatians 5:22-23)
- Ask God for wisdom in financial matters, and use it (James 1:5)
- Avoid the bondage of indebtedness (Proverbs 22:7)

The following are practical principles that apply the biblical principles already discussed:

Learn to buy wisely.

Buy with cash. Not only will this help you avoid credit, but it may also allow you to buy at a discount. Because merchants have to pay a percentage to the card company and may still wait thirty days for their money, many small merchants will accept a lower price if you offer them cash.

Separate your needs from your desires.

Don't let anyone else create a need for you. Teach yourself and your children how to evaluate advertising. Pray about this together, if necessary. Discuss the family budget with your children.

Never buy on impulse.

Anticipate your needs, and exercise patience.

Take time to compare.

Buy value, not necessarily price.

Repair instead of replace.

Always buy at your initiative. Never let anyone sell you anything until you are ready to buy. Take as much time as you need.

Seek God's guidance and help (James 1:5).

Seek counsel from others (Proverbs 15:22).

Take enough time.

The plans of the diligent lead to profit

as surely as haste leads to poverty. (Proverbs 21:5)

BALANCING WORK AND REST[1]

Whatever you do, work at it with all your heart, as working for the Lord, not for men.

COLOSSIANS 3:23

HOW DOES GOD VIEW WORK?

God is a worker. God worked to create the world, and He works to sustain it. He is also constantly at work fulfilling His purposes in history and in the life of each person (Deuteronomy 11:1-7; Philippians 2:12-13). God can only do things that are inherently good. So, the fact that God calls what He does "work" and calls that work "good" means that work has intrinsic worth.

God created man and woman in His image as a worker. Before the Fall, God assigned men and women the task of ruling His earthly creation and cultivating the garden they lived in (Genesis 1:26-29; 2:8,15). Work itself is not a result of the Fall.

Work is a gift to us. By assigning work to Adam and Eve, God was making them significant, important. By working they reflected God's image. Even after the Fall work is seen as a gift from God: "Every man who eats and drinks sees good in all his labor—it is the gift of God" (Ecclesiastes 3:13, NASB).

We were created as coworkers with God. God planted the garden; humankind cultivated it. The first partnership! This doesn't imply that God needs us to accomplish His work. Rather, because He gets exquisite pleasure from relating to His creatures, He chooses to have us participate in His plans.

WHAT ARE THE IMPLICATIONS FOR ME OF GOD'S VIEW OF WORK?

All legitimate work is an extension of God's work. Legitimate work is that which contributes to what God wants done in the world and does not actively contribute to what He does not want done. Work that destroys God's creation is a corruption of God's work. But although evil does affect even legitimate work, the work itself is good and a contribution to God's ends.

The connection between the work we do and how it contributes to God's work is not always obvious. The belief that God is mostly concerned with religious pursuits is based on four false assumptions:

- God is far more interested in people's souls than their bodies.
- The things of eternity are far more important than the things of time.
- Life itself is divided into the sacred and the secular.
- Ministers and missionaries are more important to God's program than people in "secular" jobs.

The Bible makes it clear that God is interested in whole people, not just in souls. Therefore, the person who is manufacturing trucking pallets that help get food to your breakfast table is contributing just as much to God's work as a teacher, nurse, or missionary.

Further, what goes on both in eternity and in time is real and important to God. Being colaborers with God in making His physical, temporal universe run smoothly glorifies Him just as much as colaboring with Him in evangelism. It's true that eternity is our ultimate destiny, and that our destiny should affect everything we do today. Yet this means glorifying God in every possible way—in our work as well as in our prayer, worship, and talking about the gospel. If God has designed you to be an architect or a carpenter, then building buildings to the glory of God now is one of the best ways God has given you of telling everyone that your life looks ahead—and theirs should too—toward an eternity with God.

There is no need to be bored or feel insignificant. Work is one of the main ways we fulfill the two great commandments to love. Through work we love God and others by:

- Serving people
- Meeting our own needs
- Meeting our family's needs
- Earning money to give to others
- Colaboring with God at a task He wants done

When we realize that God has placed us in a job to contribute to His creation, however mundanely, it lends a sense of dignity and destiny to our work.

Good work is an essential feature of spreading the gospel in your daily life. God has commissioned all Christians as witnesses to the truth of the gospel. But talking about Christ is not the only aspect of Christian witness. Our words mean nothing if they are not backed up by lives that reflect commitment to Jesus' two great commandments: Love God and love other people (Matthew 22:34-40). One of the primary ways we show love for God is by colaboring with Him in caring for His physical creation—by reflecting the image of God in useful work. And one of the primary ways we show love for others is by doing work that contributes to their well-being. When people see us doing our jobs with integrity and concern for both the people and the product, we earn their respect and their interest in what motivates us.

For most of us, the workplace is our chief mission field. But the task we do is not secondary to the "real" work of making friends and proclaiming the gospel. Rather, doing our work well is one of the main ways we demonstrate the gospel and glorify God.

Your career doesn't define who you are. In God's eyes, the ultimate purpose of work is to glorify God by colaboring with Him and serving others. Success in life is measured more by how well we have loved than by work status. God is interested in the heart, not the outward appearance. And while God applauds doing what it takes to get the job done (hard work, efficiency, planning), nothing justifies bending morals or hurting people.

People are driven to doing "whatever it takes" because they think their career defines them. But a Christian's identity is as a child of God, a colaborer and coheir with Christ.

> What good is it for a man to gain the whole world [a top career
> and a fat salary], and yet lose or forfeit his very self [his identity,
> his real value, his belonging to God]? (Luke 9:25)

Finding your identity in Christ liberates you from the futility and hopelessness of forever trying to climb the ladder of career success in order to prove your worth.

Winning isn't the only thing. Our job is to do God's work, God's way, and to trust Him with the results. In His sovereignty, He may allow us to experience adversity or success to mature us and show the world how we handle either one. But always, He has everything.

HOW HAS SIN AFFECTED WORK?

Sin did not destroy the dignity and value of work. When Adam and Eve sinned, God cursed the ground Adam had to cultivate, but the task of cultivating the ground was not a punishment (Genesis 3:14-19).

Sin makes work harder. God cursed the ground—the sweat, toil, and burdensomeness of work are the products of the Fall.

Sin rendered life and its work "futile." Ecclesiastes 2:18–6:9 details how even our greatest achievements in work are fleeting and ultimately futile. Last year's great innovation is obsolete this year; food has to be constantly replanted, reprocessed, and retransported; laundry and dishes are never done. Even evangelism and training disciples is a never-ending job that a pastor or missionary must constantly start over. The futility of work is one of the chief causes of frustration and burnout. Yet instead of despairing, we should celebrate the brief moments of real achievement as we colabor with God, and we should focus our hope on the day when God will free His creation from futility (Ecclesiastes 5:18-20; 9:7-10; Romans 8:1-39).

Sin affects our coworkers and the system. People lie, short-change clients, steal from employers, and destroy each other in ambitious power plays. Even Christians who want to work with integrity are forced to buy from suppliers whose ethics are shabby, so Christians indirectly support doers of evil. And even Christians who try to work with integrity are tempted to laziness or selfish ambition.

Because of sin, none of our work completely fulfills God's intentions. However, it is essential to ask ourselves whether what we are doing is the best contribution we can make to God's work.

WHAT ARE SOME GOOD AND BAD MOTIVES FOR WORKING?

Good motives include:

- Serving Christ
- Meeting people's needs
- Glorifying the Creator

Bad motives include:

- Merely collecting your paycheck, without concern for the quality of what you do

- Lust for wealth
- Lust for status, respect, or power
- Avoiding stresses in your family
- Proving to a person that you have value

It's worthwhile to prayerfully examine your motives for working. Ask God to reveal the goals and attitudes that are really in your heart. Confess any sinful motivations, and ask God to forgive you, heal you, and enable you to take on godly motives.

HOW SHOULD I DEAL WITH THE SIN I FIND IN MY WORKPLACE?

You can't eradicate it, nor can you escape it. "Do not be shocked," says Ecclesiastes 5:8 (NASB), when you see evil at work. Christ died to save and transform workers, but until His second coming, people and systems will remain corrupt, and work will still be futile.

Don't flee to Christian businesses—God wants you to be His witness in the midst of a sinful world, and even Christian organizations are composed of sinners. Instead, pray for wisdom and compassion as you live in a flawed world.

You can let Christ transform you, one worker. You can let Christ restore your relationship to God, transform your character into one that reflects His integrity and love, and turn your approach to work into one that serves Him.

Slaves, obey your earthly masters in everything; and do it, not only when their eye is on you and to win their favor, but with sincerity of heart and reverence for the Lord. Whatever you do, work at it with all your heart, as working for the Lord, not for men, since you know that you will receive an inheritance from the Lord as a reward. It is the Lord Christ you are serving. (Colossians 3:22-24)

Paul wrote these words to people who did menial work every day, and who had no freedom to change jobs or escape harsh masters. He also had words for masters (and other supervisors):

Masters, provide your slaves with what is right and fair, because you know that you also have a Master in heaven. (Colossians 4:1)

Christ is your Boss. Work to please Him, and feel His pleasure when you do.

"Hate what is evil; cling to what is good. . . . Do not be overcome by evil, but overcome evil with good" (Romans 12:9,21). This does not mean we are to be moral policemen, pointing out everyone's faults. Rather, we can overcome evil by doing the best possible jobs, by resisting temptations to despair and judge others, and by trusting God to handle the evildoers.

God is sovereign. Although a situation may be out of your control, it is never out of God's control. He is all-loving and all-powerful. Someday He will eradicate all evil from this world. Until then, even when you feel helpless and confused about why God is allowing something, you can pray. Jesus exhorts us to pray and not lose heart (Luke 18:1-8), knowing that God will take into account our persistent, trusting prayers.

If there are other Christians in your company, you might try meeting weekly, not to talk but to pray.

God uses evil.

> Consider it pure joy, my brothers, whenever you face trials of many kinds, because you know that the testing of your faith develops perseverance. Perseverance must finish its work so that you may be mature and complete, not lacking anything. (James 1:2-4)

People who survive the jungle of the workplace do so by letting God use it to transform them.

You must take action if you are called upon to do what is wrong. Distinguish between direct and indirect participation in evil. A grocer cannot help selling food to people who have obtained their money through crime and will commit more crime by the strength obtained through that food. But you are responsible to act to correct an evil when your job calls for direct participation in what you know to be wrong. To lie to a customer, to cheat the government, to steal from a vendor, or to ignore the laws that govern your industry violates Scripture—you must refuse to do such things.

You should act when your own conscience is violated. Take time to make a moral decision whenever your conscience sounds an alarm. Look for clear scriptural grounds for making your decision, then take deliberate steps to avoid evil and promote good.

You should act when it is in your power to end or avoid evil. You may not be as uninfluential as you think. Look and pray for areas in which you can make a difference.

You should act when innocent people stand to be affected by evil.

Go to the source, if possible. Talk with the person who seems to be the problem. Don't quote Scripture at him if he is not a Christian; instead, appeal to broad categories of morality and justice. If the source is a condition rather than a person, go to the person with the power to do something about ending the evil. Take with you suggestions about what this person might do. Don't adopt a condemning attitude; rather, ask questions, bring out important facts, challenge people to do what is right, and at least raise the issue of integrity.

Join the battle in the area where you feel you can be most effective. Use your God-given abilities, personality, resources, and relationships. You may not have the power yourself, but you may be the kind of person whom warring parties or a particular individual will take seriously. You may be the only person with the guts to say what no one else is saying, or to stand by someone who faces a critical but difficult decision.

Seek limited, measurable gains. You may not be able to change the practices of an entire industry, but you may be able to find a shrewd alternative for your own company. Be creative in finding options that are more ethical but just as productive.

Expect positive results but also some negative ones. Count the cost. The risk could be too great. But if the issue is important enough, take the risk.

If necessary, leave. Leaving should be your last resort, for God values endurance. Yet, because He also values integrity, you may have to leave if remaining would require you to participate directly in evil. In that case, trust God to take care of you and your family because you are obeying Him.

HOW SHOULD I CHOOSE A JOB?

God designed you with certain talents and interests (Psalm 139:13-16). The way He designed you is a clue to the service He desires you to perform in His world. Take stock of what you like to do and can do well. Think and pray about what motivates you to constructive ends (the pleasure of producing something well made, of seeing justice prevail, or of seeing people change for the better).

Follow the steps of right decision making. (See pages 153–154.)

Don't assume that "spiritual" vocations are more important to God than "secular" jobs. God is concerned about all kinds of needs. He loves and values people in secular jobs just as much as those in professional "ministry." If God has gifted you for full-time vocational ministry, then do it. If not, don't try to earn personal significance by going into a "spiritual" career.

Pray for wisdom, seek counsel, then choose. Nothing will make the choice for you. Trust God's guidance, but expect a level of uncertainty about whether this is the "right" job that God has "called" you to. God is bigger than your mistakes.

HOW SHOULD I VIEW LEISURE AND REST?

Chronic busyness and crushing boredom are both signs that we lack God's perspective on work and rest.

God gives us a purpose. If your identity is rooted in relating to God, then you won't try to make work fill your need for meaning in life. Boredom envelops you when you feel that what you are doing is pointless. Busyness engulfs you when you strive to make your life count because you don't think you matter unless you are producing.

God gives us rest. Because our work is God's work, and because He is ultimately responsible for the results, He gives us the freedom to leave it, to trust Him with it, and to enjoy some rest in life. Christians who feel guilty when they relax believe deep down that (1) God either cannot or will not provide for their needs, and so (2) they must therefore provide for their own needs, mostly through their work. The only way out is to stop working for self (in anxiety and fear) and start working for God (in trust and peace). Rest—freedom from work—actually begins at work, when we stop relying on the job and start trusting Jesus to supply our needs (Matthew 11:28-30).

On the other hand, people who survive the work week longing for the weekend may believe that their work has no value, that the only purpose in life is to enjoy the pleasure of leisure. They need to know that their work has divine value.

They also need to see that God gives us rest in order to refresh us to fulfill His purposes in work; He didn't give work in order to finance our leisure (Exodus 20:9-10). Recreation is for re-creating us into whole people physically, mentally, and spiritually in order that we may serve God better.

God gave Israel one day of rest out of seven. Some Christians ignore this principle, filling up Saturday and Sunday with all the things they didn't have time to do during the week. Others turn the Sabbath into a legalistic requirement, filling Sunday with church activities because they think God demands one day in seven and that this means church involvement. However, the New Testament attitude toward the Sabbath seems to be that on one day out of seven we rest from our toil to acknowledge that while God has given us work, He is the ultimate Provider of our needs. It makes sense that we should spend time on that day celebrating and worshipping God, as well as enjoying the rest He gives.

Cultivate interests and commitments outside of work. Cultivate interests that express aspects of yourself that don't come out at work. "My work is my hobby" reflects the narrow life of a person who is striving to earn meaning in his life by work. God has purpose for you also in a personal relationship with Him, in family relationships, in involvement with other Christians, in responsibilities to your community, and in relationships with non-Christians. Spend some time praying and thinking about how to glorify God in the personal, family, church, community, and work areas of your life. But don't be too serious—build rest and fun into all these areas.

BEING A CHRISTIAN IN SOCIETY

Do not repay anyone evil for evil. Be careful to do what is right in the eyes of everybody. If it is possible, as far as it depends on you, live at peace with everyone.

ROMANS 12:17-18

WHAT ARE MY RESPONSIBILITIES IN SECULAR SOCIETY?
Pray.

I urge, then, first of all, that requests, prayers, intercession and thanksgiving be made for everyone—for kings and all those in authority, that we may live peaceful and quiet lives in all godliness and holiness. (1 Timothy 2:1-2)

The king's heart is in the hand of the LORD;
    he directs it like a watercourse wherever he pleases.
      (Proverbs 21:1)

No matter how secular the government, God is in control. He often allows foolish leaders to make foolish decisions and bring judgment on themselves. Yet God answers the prayers of godly citizens. Ask Him persistently to give your leaders wisdom and humility. Ask for leaders who know God and love justice. Pray about specific political issues.

Submit to legitimate authority. To Christians under an authoritarian pagan regime, Paul wrote:

> Everyone must submit himself to the governing authorities, for there is no authority except that which God has established. . . . Consequently, he who rebels against the authority is rebelling against what God has instituted, and those who do so will bring judgment on themselves. For rulers hold no terror for those who do right, but for those who do wrong. Do you want to be free from fear of the one in authority? Then do what is right and he will commend you. . . .
>
> This is also why you pay taxes, for the authorities are God's servants, who give their full time to governing. Give everyone what you owe him: If you owe taxes, pay taxes; if revenue, then revenue; if respect, then respect; if honor, then honor. (Romans 13:1-3,6-7)

Put God first. For Paul and other early Christians, submitting to the authorities sometimes meant accepting punishment for proclaiming the gospel when it was forbidden. They rejected armed rebellion, but they could not obey an order to do what God forbade or cease what God commanded (Acts 4:1-20; 5:27-32; 16:1-40). They preferred prison and execution to denying Christ. But their respectful attitudes and otherwise law-abiding lives made them credible witnesses for Christ when arrested for Christian activities.

Seek justice.

The righteous care about justice for the poor,
> but the wicked have no such concern. (Proverbs 29:7)

Justice is:

- Each person getting his due (Job 34:10-12; Romans 13:7)
- Conforming to true, consistent standards (Leviticus 19:35-36; Isaiah 28:17)

Christians should promote laws and legal decisions that give people what they deserve and conform to biblical standards of rightness. Honest measures, fair wages for honest work, fair prices, truthful advertising, punishment or restitution that fits the crime, impartial courts, thoughtful stewardship over the environment, concern for future generations, protection of property—Christians should uphold all these.

God commanded the Israelites not only to act with justice and obey the laws, but also to help defenseless people to obtain justice. Resident aliens, the innocent, and the poor were singled out as people who needed legal advocates.

Participate. Christians in democratic countries have rights unimaginable to the first believers. We can vote, petition, protest, organize, speak in city councils, and run for office. These rights vastly increase our ability to promote justice. At the very least, all citizens of democracies should educate themselves about the issues and the candidates and vote whenever possible. You can particularly make a difference in local elections and decisions, where only a small number of people participate.

The separation of church and state means that the organized church can't integrate with the government. However, your personal theological belief can and should affect the political process. To be salt and light in the world (Matthew 5:13-16) means influencing society for God's truth in every way possible.

Respect those whose views differ. Christians generally agree about political goals (decreasing poverty, preserving the earth from destruction, preventing war and oppression, encouraging economic prosperity, reducing crime), but they differ as to the methods they think are wise. When you disagree with a Christian (or a non-Christian) about politics, assume that he or she has good motives unless proven otherwise. Discuss the biblical standards with, listen to, and love him. Pray together, if you can.

NOTES

DISCOVERING THE CHARACTER OF GOD

1. Most of the material in answer to the question "Who is God?" comes from J. I. Packer, "God," *The New Dictionary of Theology*, ed. Sinclair B. Ferguson, David B. Wright, and J. I. Packer (Downers Grove, IL: InterVarsity, 1988), 275–277.
2. Packer, "God," 276.
3. Packer, "God," 277.
4. Packer, "Holy Spirit," *The New Dictionary*, 316.
5. Jerry Bridges, *True Community: The Biblical Practice of Koinonia* (Colorado Springs, CO: NavPress, 2012), 90.
6. I. Howard Marshall, *The Acts of the Apostles: An Historical Commentary: Tyndale New Testament Series* (Grand Rapids, MI: Eerdmans, 1980), 69.
7. C. S. Lewis, *Mere Christianity* (New York: Macmillan, 1960 [1943]), 86–87.

LEARNING ABOUT PRAYER

1. R. Loren Sandford, *Birthing the Church* (South Plainfield, NJ: Bridge Publishing Company, 1984), 67–69.
2. Warren Myers and Ruth Myers, *Praise: A Door to God's Presence* (Colorado Springs, CO: NavPress, 1987), 14.
3. Myers and Myers, 11.
4. C. S. Lewis, *Reflections on the Psalms* (London: Collins, 1967), 79.
5. Lewis, *Reflections*, 81.
6. Myers and Myers, 9–20.
7. C. S. Lewis, *Letters to Malcolm: Chiefly on Prayer* (New York: Harcourt, Brace, Jovanovich, 1963, 1964), 32–34.
8. Lewis, *Letters*, 52.
9. Lewis, *Letters*, 60.

10. Lewis, *Letters*, 53.

11. Lewis, *Letters*, 66.

12. Anthony Bloom, *Living Prayer* (Springfield, IL: Templegate Publishers, 1966), 90–91.

13. Bloom, 91.

HAVING AN EFFECTIVE QUIET TIME

1. Warren Myers and Ruth Myers, *Pray: How to Be Effective in Prayer* (Colorado Springs, CO: NavPress, 1983), 146.

DEPENDING ON GOD

1. Much of this explanation is drawn from Jerry Bridges, *True Community: The Biblical Practice of Koinonia* (Colorado Springs, CO: NavPress, 2012), 27–32.

GETTING THE MOST FROM THE BIBLE

1. Lavonne Neff, *Practical Christianity: The Down-to-Earth Guide to Heavenly Living* (Wheaton, IL: Tyndale, 1987), 384.

2. Neff, 385.

3. Adapted from Richard Warren, *Twelve Dynamic Bible Study Methods* (Wheaton, IL: Scripture Press Publications, 1981), 35.

4. Anthony Bloom, *Living Prayer* (Springfield, IL: Templegate Publishers, 1966), 53.

5. Warren, 34.

DEFINING IMPORTANT CHRISTIAN TERMS

1. Leon Morris, "Atonement," *The New Dictionary of Theology*, ed. Sinclair B. Ferguson, David B. Wright, and J. I. Packer (Downers Grove, IL: InterVarsity, 1988), 54–57.

2. M. J. Harris, "Death," *The New Dictionary of Theology*, 188.

3. W. Schmithals, "Death," *The New International Dictionary of New Testament Theology*, vol. 1, ed. Colin Brown (Grand Rapids, MI: Zondervan, 1975), 353–359.

4. G. W. Martin, "Faith," *The New Dictionary of Theology*, 246.

5. Harris, "Immortality," *The New Dictionary of Theology*, 332–333.

6. Harris, "Intermediate State," *The New Dictionary of Theology*, 339–340.

7. N. T. Wright, "Righteousness," *The New Dictionary of Theology*, 591.

8. Klaus Bockmuehl, "Sanctification," *The New Dictionary of Theology*, 613.

STARTING A SMALL GROUP

1. Jerry Bridges, *True Community: The Biblical Practice of Koinonia* (Colorado Springs, CO: NavPress, 2012), 71.

DISCERNING GOD'S WILL

1. The definitions of the three kinds of God's will are from Garry Friesen and J. Robin Maxson, *Decision Making and the Will of God* (Portland, OR: Multnomah, 1980), 32–36. Friesen is the leading current proponent of the view that God does not have an individual will for each person's life. His book analyzes both views and is a good first book on the subject. For a thorough treatment of the opposing view, see Dr. Charles F. Stanley, *How to Listen to God* (Nashville: Oliver-Nelson, 1985).

2. J. I. Packer, *Knowing God* (Downers Grove, IL: InterVarsity, 1973), 80.

3. Freisen and Maxson, 197. Their advice on learning and operating by wisdom is valuable whether or not you think God has an individual will for your life.

MAKING MORAL DECISIONS

1. Gary Friesen and J. Robin Maxson, *Decision Making and the Will of God* (Portland, OR: Multnomah, 1980), 381. Much of this teaching is based on Friesen's approach.

2. Friesen and Maxson, 420–421.

3. John Donne, "Meditation 17," *John Donne: Poetry and Prose*, ed. Frank J. Warnke (New York: Random House, 1967), 339, spelling updated.

DEALING WITH EMOTIONS
1. James C. Dobson, *Emotions: Can You Trust Them?* (Ventura, CA: Gospel Light, 1980), 18.

THINKING ABOUT DATING
1. Adapted from Stacy Rinehart and Paula Rinehart, *Choices: Finding God's Way in Dating, Sex, Singleness, and Marriage* (Colorado Springs, CO: NavPress, 1982), 29–85.

STAYING SEXUALLY PURE
1. Several of the points in this list come from James C. Dobson, *Dr. Dobson Answers Your Questions* (Wheaton, IL: Tyndale, 1982), 438.
2. Stacy and Paula Rinehart, *Choices: Finding God's Way in Dating, Sex, Singleness, and Marriage* (Colorado Springs, CO: NavPress, 1982), 92.
3. Adapted from Rinehart and Rinehart, 112–115.
4. Many of these differences come from Dobson, 405–411.

HONORING GOD IN MARRIAGE
1. Ralph Martin, *Husbands, Wives, Parents, Children: Foundations for the Christian Family* (Ann Arbor, MI: Servant, 1978, 1983), 23.
2. Martin, 23.
3. Martin, 24–25.
4. James C. Dobson, *Love for a Lifetime* (Portland, OR: Multnomah, 1986), 107–111.
5. C. S. Lewis, *Mere Christianity* (New York: Macmillan, [1960], 1943), 96.

REARING CHILDREN
1. Ralph Martin, *Husbands, Wives, Parents, Children: Foundations for the Christian Family* (Ann Arbor, MI: Servant, 1978, 1983), 133.

2. Answers for this question are taken from Mary White, *Growing Together: Building Your Family's Spiritual Life* (Colorado Springs, CO: NavPress, 1981).

MANAGING MONEY
1. The material in this chapter is adapted from Jake Barnett, *Wealth and Wisdom* (Colorado Springs, CO: NavPress, 1987).
2. Barnett, 256.

BALANCING WORK AND REST
1. The material in this chapter is adapted from Doug Sherman and William Hendricks, *Your Work Matters to God* (Colorado Springs, CO: NavPress, 1987).

ABOUT THE AUTHOR

Former senior editor of Bible Studies at NavPress and author of more than fifty study guides, **Karen Lee-Thorp** has spent almost two decades exploring how people grow spiritually. Her books include *A Compact Guide to the Bible*, *How to Ask Great Questions*, and *Why Beauty Matters*, and she was the series editor for the LIFECHANGE Bible study series. Karen is a graduate of Yale University. She speaks to women's groups and writes from her home in Brea, California.